More WISDOM in Failure

notionpress.com

MORE WISDOM IN FAILURE

CHIMGAEMEZU MORRISON

notionpress.com

Notion Press

Old No. 38, New No. 6

McNichols Road, Chetpet

Chennai - 600 031

First Published by Notion Press 2015

ISBN 978-93-5206-426-7

To the monarch and the King of the Universe, "God Almighty."
To my parents rev. (Rt. Sp.) Morrison Onyechefulam and Mrs
Josephine Nwanyiwuaku Emetuo.

PREFACE

More Wisdom in Failure is a self-help book written to bring hope to the souls of many around the world. It is an educating, entertaining and motivating book for the reader. "More Wisdom in Failure" is written by the author from his own experiences in life.

ACKNOWLEDGEMENTS

I would like to express my gratitude to the people who saw me through the process of writing this book; to all those who provided support, talked things over, read, wrote, and offered comments in the course of my writing this book.

Special thanks to MR. JUDE OMO for his immense effort, encouragement and guidance in making sure that this book was published. Thank you, sir for giving me all the time and attention that I needed in making this dream a reality.

Big thanks to Mr. Chandra Kumar who was the architect behind publishing this book. You are the best foreign friend I have ever had!

I would like to thank all my friends who have been there for me from the time I started this journey and all those who truly believed in me.

"REMAIN BLESSED..!

CONTENTS

Preface *vii*

Acknowledgements *ix*

1. A Good Listener 1
2. Mr Trouble and Mr Problem 3
3. Mr Fear 7
4. You Must be a Champion 31
5. Don't Give a Reason! Look for a Way 33
6. The Hand that is on Top (A Giver) 41
7. Change Your Mind Set 43
8. See Through my View 47
9. Power of Words 51
10. Anger 53
11. A Set Time 55
12. Big Mama Success 61
13. Dream 63
14. Life Purpose / Journey of Life 69
15. Compliments 75
16. Them Say 83
17. What Money can Do! 85
18. How Wonderfully God Can Bless a Country 89
19. The Power of the Mind! 97

20. A Complainant 105
21. Observe a Change 109
22. A Winner 115
23. A Good Observer 117
24. Don't be Greedy 119
25. Can You Stop Crime? 121
26. How Careful Can a Man Be?? 141
27. Time 145

1. A GOOD LISTENER

a. A good listener gives his full attention and concentration while someone is speaking.
b. A good listener doesn't allow anything to be a distraction while someone is speaking.
c. A good listener does not argue because arguments may make the speaker forget what he intends to say, or to speak lesser than intended.
d. A good listener does not interrupt while someone speaks.
e. A good listener doesn't shuffle papers while someone is speaking.
f. A good listener looks interested, and helps make the speaker feel relaxed.
g. A good listener doesn't look around elsewhere while someone is speaking to him.
h. A good listener has words of compliment to the speaker.
i. A good listener doesn't criticize the speaker because if he does, it would throw the speaker off balance.
j. A good listener cheers the speaker up to make him feel superior. For instance, how will you feel when you are speaking and people listening to you are saying: "RIDE ON SIR, WE ARE HEARING YOU", and "MOVE ON WE ARE WITH YOU!" Do you know that it gives the speaker the spirit to flow on the stage?
k. A good listener always wait for the appropriate time to ask questions.

When we talk about listening to God, (The Creator of the Universe), remember, He doesn't talk to your physical ears. Some bad listeners may say: "I never get any response from Him. I don't hear anything from Him, What do I do?" He does speak to every soul he has created on a regular basis. One can complain of not hearing or receiving any response from Him because the person himself is a bad listener. There is no one in this world that does not have the consciousness of the creator of the universe. A few try to deny His existence, but when you practice listening well, you will enjoy His thoughts, directions and opinions on anything concerning your life. Be a good listener. Listening with your heart and spirit. If you meditate and start listening with your ears, you may not hear anything. This is because He communicates with your spirit. When you talk with Him, He will respond to you, but you have to listen with your spirit.

DON'T FORGET THAT IT PAYS TO BE A GOOD LISTERNER. THIS IS ANOTHER WAY TO BE A GOOD LISTENER SOON.

2. MR TROUBLE AND MR PROBLEM

Before I proceed, I would like to MAKE YOU UNDERSTAND that TROUBLE and PROBLEM are not the same things. Mr. TROUBLE and Mr. PROBLEM may sound the same but are actually different. So, don't mix them up. Who is Mr. TROUBLE? Let me give you the reply I got from Mr. TROUBLE.

a. Mr. Trouble told me that he comes in disguise in the midst of peace.
b. He is the only one who can plant the seed of:
   - Confusion
   - Catastrophe
   - War
   - Tribal misunderstanding
   - State of emergency
   - Backbiting
   - Envy

MR. TROUBLE cannot be measured and qualified as small or big. The earth is filled with good things for our consumption, yet we are not advised to eat all of it. This is because some things are for our advantage and some are for our disadvantage. How does this happen?

For instance, if you have only a positive wire running in your home, how do you expect current to flow? In your mind, will a positive charge alone produce current? To get current for usage, you must have positive and negative charge. Don't run away from the bad. Don't make or look for MR TROUBLE. If he comes looking for you, face him and conquer him. When you do that, you will be able to conquer him tomorrow if he returns.

NOTE: Everything in life has advantages and disadvantages but what makes a thing advantageous is when its advantages are greater than its disadvantages.

Advantages of Trouble

- It creates room for learning by teaching you things in hard way.
- It will help you know who your enemies really are.
- It will make you wiser.
- It will make you know your strength.
- It will harden your heart for challenges ahead. i.e., by making you tougher
- It gives you room to predict what someone can do.
- It gives you room to prove yourself as the hero or champion.
- It helps strengthen your power of reasoning and thoughts by moving forward

Disadvantages of Mr.trouble

- It can result in death.
- It can result in shedding of innocent blood
- Many things are in disorder because of trouble. You may spend years to build something and it is destroyed in a minute.
- Some take advantage to display their wickedness against a so-called enemy.
- It is a time of destruction
- It causes lots of wastage
- It causes hatred and causes people to think of revenge.
- Your heart tends towards destruction.

Mr. Problem

Mr. PROBLEM is a challenge. Mr. PROBLEM merely means a challenge that faces you as an opposition. It is Mrs. Teacher in another form. You can call her a muscle-builder or gym.

MR PROBLEM builds you up in many ways mentally, emotionally, socially, financially; spiritually and otherwise. When you face MR PROBLEM and defeat him, you are a hero. Don't you know that there is no hero without a challenge? Every athlete competes for a championship to be a champion. The championship is the challenge. When you defeat it, you become the CHAMPION! When you face a challenge in life, don't speak bad. Your words have the power to do anything. We know that anything is possible in life. The words we vocalize have the capacity to change our situation. Don't run away from challenges. It has the capacity of making you what you should be. Your challenge can keep you ahead if you know how to deal with it when it comes. Develop the habit of welcoming Mr. PROBLEM whenever he knocks. Don't run away from it. Face it. Remember that he fights and runs away, and lives to fight another day. If you don't conquer it, it is an unfinished fight. That means that the fight is still waiting for you. A challenge is a problem that you face at any point in time.

For instance, someone who has not had food for a long time will definitely have a different prayer in mind. The desire and craving for food is an immediate need. But, it will be absurd to think that in that state, he will be craving for a car or asking for a bike when he does not have the strength as a result of hunger. The challenge in this case is hunger. A lady who is due for marriage and does not have hope of a man proposing to her or her proposing to a man worries. Marriage becomes a challenge. When she prays, she will ask for marriage. Even if there are thousands of men around she can't get married to just anyone. A guy in prison prays for his freedom. When you enter prison, only then will you know what freedom means.

I once visited a friend, Roy, in hospital. Roy is a good friend and we grew up together. He always tells me about a business deal that he is waiting to execute, and enjoins me to always pray for it. Abruptly, once, Roy fell ill and was taken to hospital. When I saw Roy, lying there, critically ill, I felt so sad. I asked him, "What should I do for you?" Roy asked me to pray to God to heal him. "But what about that business you told me? I thought those men were coming next week?" I asked. Roy said, "Please pray to God that He should take the business and heal me!" I thought to myself that maybe his sickness had affected Roy's sense of reasoning. How could Roy forget the business he has long anticipated? It was nonsense.

But, that was exactly what Roy needed. Before his illness, he used to tell me that he was going to buy an Angelina SUV and a land ROVER discovery SUV for himself and his fiancée. When we were talking in the hospital, I wanted to hear him say to God that he wanted those cars. But instead, he was asking for his healing. That made me realise that his need was a challenge, and his want was a choice. (When you need something badly and can't get it or solve it, and someone happens to give you something that looks like it, it helps. For instance, say you needed to cross a swampy area with shoes. If you don't wear shoes, your feet may get dirty or wounded. You don't have shoes of your own. Suddenly, someone gifted you rain boots. So what do you do? You will use them. You won't say that they aren't the appropriate shoes - your necessity demands that you use them. The shoes were given to you when you needed them. The need for the shoes was met but the choice was not met. Later, when you have an occasion in mind and prefer something different to wear, it becomes a want.

At the time when you were about to cross that swampy area, and you needed shoes, the shoes brought to you were not rejected because it was what you needed. The shoes were given to you and you didn't mind if it was your size or not, you didn't care about the colour or make. Your challenge was to cross that swampy area and a shoe was needed. Your ability to do more than the ordinary to meet situations matters. You don't get WANTS from people having pity on you. You can get your NEEDS. For instance, a beggar comes to you for help. Do you give them what he WANTS? No. You give them what he NEEDS. The essential needs of a man are:

a. Food
b. Clothing
c. Shelter.

Let's say a beggar begs for something beyond the essentials. Let's say he asks for a car. Will you give a beggar a car? No. The reason is that a car is not a need, but a WANT. It is not a challenge. He could enter a train, bus, or taxi on the road to anywhere. But if he asks for food, even if you don't have food, or are not capable of providing food at that time, you can give him money to buy him food. When you do this, you meet his need and not his want. Food, at that point in time, was his major challenge. Thus, a challenge is a problem.

3. MR FEAR

Fear is an unpleasant emotion caused by the threat of danger, pain or harm. It could be expressed as being afraid of someone or something, as likely to be dangerous, painful, or harmful.

MR FEAR is dangerous in life. He takes you out of a place where you could have won.

Fear can take you to a place of failure in the name of protection. Fear's home seems safer than anywhere else, in his eyes. Fear is married to poverty, and doesn't want problems, but rather likes the state he is in. He complains, procrastinates and is an enemy of risk. Science calls MR FEAR a scalar quantity as it has magnitude but no direction. I was lucky to sit with MR FEAR in a conference. After the conference, I seized the opportunity to ask him some questions. I asked, "Mr. Fear, who are you and what is your mission here?

"I am FALSE EVIDENCE APPEARING to be REAL."

"Are you telling that you are not truth?" I asked.

MR FEAR replied, "Of course! How can false evidence be true?"

"Really?" I shouted. "Now what is your mission here?"

F = False

E = Evidence

A = Appearing

R = Real

I force people out of the place where they could have won. I make people who believe in me to be poor. I make people get defeated. I show people bad roads that appear like good roads because they believe me. Men believe me and I take advantage of them and make sure that I bring them closer to my wife, Mrs. Poverty to cook a delicious meal for them. I am MR FEAR I respect nobody. I don't fear man. Man has a will to choose. If they choose me, fine. I never force anyone. After all, God gave them the gift of choice and if, by omission or by commission, they choose me, how can I have rejected them? I have strong feelings that you men must have discussed me so much that you even dream of having the opportunity to meet me face to face. My regards to your people! Please my good friend, when you go home. Tell people not to visit my home because my home is dangerous!"

He knows the way but can't drive the car. He can give proper guidance on how to get it but ask him to get it himself, and he cannot. He is like a man who is outside the stadium when the players play and he shouts at them saying that they don't know how to play. Put him there, he doesn't know how to play himself. A head full of fear has no place for dreams. Leave MR FEAR alone and make a choice and go for it. Deal with MR FEAR. (Prophet David who once lived on this earth said, "Though I walk through the valley of the shadow of Death, I will fear no evil for you are with me. Your rod and your staff comfort me!" MR FEAR is a network service put by the devil for you not to get to your destiny.

What Mr Fear can do to you When You Allow Him

1. Bring failure.
2. Make you crawl.
3. Gives you the impression that you can't make it in life.
4. Make you to feel defeated.
5. Make you accept loss.
6. Takes you away from where you could have won.
7. Make you not understand your own stand.
8. Remind you of your past mistakes.
9. Make you to discover who you really are.
10. Destroy greatness.
11. Make you remain where you are.
12. Put you in a holdup
13. Lock you up in prison for life.
14. Make you complain

Don't forget that the solution of fear is inbuilt in you.

How to Stop the Effect of Mr Fear

MR FEAR can ruin the quality of life. MR FEAR can be visualized in different ways. It is an afflictive feeling of impending danger or risk. It is a warning that makes you understand your limitations in life. There was a time when MR FEAR and religion were put on an equal footing. Have you heard about early civilizations when men were food gatherers and hunters? In those eras, men associated MR FEAR with everything. They believed in Spirits, God and Nature. Fear of religion made them sacrifice wealth to satisfy the divine creator.

Popular religions such as Buddhism too are based on the concept of fear of suffering. The effects of fear had a significant role to play in the life of common men. When you move down from religious philosophy to everyday existence, you will find that these fears prevail in all aspects of life. You fear discomfort and so, you work for food and other necessities in life. No matter whether you live to eat, you will always be afraid of suffering in life. The effect of fear not only causes destruction, but also supports retrogression in life. Anger is the most significant effect of fear. You become angry when you suffer from insecurity. Stress is one of the most vital effects of fear. When you become extremely stressed and tense, you have high chances of suffering from tunnel vision, or (a condition in which things cannot be seen properly if they are not straight ahead. Fear bewilders you to such an extent that you are unable to choose the right path. However, the effects of long term fear, if you always get angry every day, you are sure to end up being angry and stressful. Some of the most common effects of fear are as follows. When you are extremely afraid, you tend to avoid particular situations in life. Fear causes insomnia. You cannot sleep at night. Fear makes you lazy and unsocial. You lack vital energy. You don't feel like working and mixing with people around you. Fear makes you avoid taking part in social gatherings. You prefer to lock yourself up in a room. Fear makes you over conscious that you always feel that someone is constantly criticizing and judging you. Fear prevents you from going to public places. You hate meeting new people and you don't like getting introduced at all. Fear indulges substance abuse too.

How can Effects of Fear be Minimized?

To eliminate effects of fear, you can take the help of effective NLP Techniques – or Neuro Linguistic Programming Techniques. It works to treat several conditions, fear and phobias. As for what MR FEAR is, biologically speaking: When a person experiences fear, certain areas in their brain such as the amygdale and the hypothalamus are activated and appear to control the first physical response to fear. Chemicals such as adrenaline and the stress hormone cortisol are released into the blood stream causing certain physical reactions such as:

- Rapid heart rate
- Increased blood pressure
- Tightening of muscles
- Sharpened or redirected senses
- Dilation of the pupils (to let in more light)
- Increased sweating]

Fear is PHOBIA

Ablutophobia - Fear of washing or bathing.

Acarophobia - Fear of itching or of the insects that cause itching.

Acerophobia - Fear of sourness.

Achluophobia - Fear of darkness.

Acousticophobia - Fear of noise.

Acrophobia - Fear of heights.

Aerophobia - Fear of drafts, air swallowing, or airborne noxious substances.

Aeroacrophobia - Fear of open high places.

Aeronausiphobia - Fear of vomiting secondary to airsickness.

Agateophobia - Fear of insanity.

Agliophobia - Fear of pain.

Agoraphobia	- Fear of open spaces or of being in crowded, public places like markets. Fear of leaving a safe place.
Agraphobia	- Fear of sexual abuse.
Agrizoophobia	- Fear of wild animals.
Agyrophobia	- Fear of streets or crossing the street.
Aichmophobia	- Fear of needles or pointed objects.
Ailurophobia	- Fear of cats.
Albuminurophobia	- Fear of kidney disease.
Alektorophobia	- Fear of chickens.
Algophobia	- Fear of pain.
Alliumphobia	- Fear of garlic.
Allodoxaphobia	- Fear of opinions.
Altophobia	- Fear of heights.
Amathophobia	- Fear of dust.
Amaxophobia	- Fear of riding in a car.
Ambulophobia	- Fear of walking.
Amnesiphobia	- Fear of amnesia.
Amychophobia	- Fear of scratches or being scratched.
Anablephobia	- Fear of looking up.
Ancraophobia	- Fear of wind. (Anemophobia)
Androphobia	- Fear of men.
Anemophobia	- Fear of air drafts or wind. (Ancraophobia)
Anginophobia	- Fear of angina, choking or narrowness.
Anglophobia	- Fear of England or English culture, etc.
Angrophobia	- Fear of anger or of becoming angry.
Ankylophobia	- Fear of immobility of a joint.
Anthrophobia or Anthophobia	- Fear of flowers.

Anthropophobia	- Fear of people or society.
Antlophobia	- Fear of floods.
Anuptaphobia	- Fear of staying single.
Apeirophobia	- Fear of infinity.
Aphenphosmphobia	- Fear of being touched. (Haphephobia)
Apiphobia	- Fear of bees.
Apotemnophobia	- Fear of persons with amputations.
Arachibutyrophobia	- Fear of peanut butter sticking to the roof of the mouth.
Arachnephobia or Arachnophobia	- Fear of spiders.
Arithmophobia	- Fear of numbers.
Arrhenphobia	- Fear of men.
Arsonphobia	- Fear of fire.
Asthenophobia	- Fear of fainting or weakness.
Astraphobia or Astrapophobia	- Fear of thunder and lightning. (Ceraunophobia, Keraunophobia)
Astrophobia	- Fear of stars or celestial space.
Asymmetriphobia	- Fear of asymmetrical things.
Ataxiophobia	- Fear of ataxia. (Muscular in - coordination)
Ataxophobia	- Fear of disorder or untidiness.
Atelophobia	- Fear of imperfection.
Atephobia	- Fear of ruin or ruins.
Athazagoraphobia	- Fear of being forgotten or ignored or forgetting.
Atomosophobia	- Fear of atomic explosions.
Atychiphobia	- Fear of failure.
Aulophobia	- Fear of flutes.

Aurophobia	- Fear of gold.
Auroraphobia	- Fear of Northern lights.
Autodysomophobia	- Fear of one who has a vile odor.
Automatonophobia	- Fear of ventriloquist's dummies, animatronic creatures, wax statues - anything that falsly represents a sentient being.
Automysophobia	- Fear of being dirty.
Autophobia	- Fear of being alone or of oneself.
Aviophobia or Aviatophobia	- Fear of flying.
Bacillophobia	- Fear of microbes.
Bacteriophobia	- Fear of bacteria.
Ballistophobia	- Fear of missiles or bullets.
Bolshephobia	- Fear of Bolsheviks.
Barophobia	- Fear of gravity.
Basophobia or Basiphobia	- Inability to stand. Fear of walking or falling.
Bathmophobia	- Fear of stairs or steep slopes.
Bathophobia	- Fear of depth.
Batophobia	- Fear of heights or being close to high buildings.
Batrachophobia	- Fear of amphibians, such as frogs, newts, salamanders, etc.
Belonephobia	- Fear of pins and needles. (Aichmophobia)
Bibliophobia	- Fear of books.
Blennophobia	- Fear of slime.
Bogyphobia	- Fear of bogeys or the bogeyman.

Botanophobia	- Fear of plants.
Bromidrosiphobia or Bromidrophobia	- Fear of body smells.
Brontophobia	- Fear of thunder and lightning.
Bufonophobia	- Fear of toads.
Ecclesiophobia	- Fear of church.
Ecophobia	- Fear of home.
Eicophobia	- Fear of home surroundings. (Domatophobia, Oikophobia)
Eisoptrophobia	- Fear of mirrors or of seeing oneself in a mirror.
Electrophobia	- Fear of electricity.
Eleutherophobia	- Fear of freedom.
Elurophobia	- Fear of cats. (Ailurophobia)
Emetophobia	- Fear of vomiting.
Enetophobia	- Fear of pins.
Enochlophobia	- Fear of crowds.
Enosiophobia or Enissophobia	- Fear of having committed an unpardonable sin or of criticism.
Entomophobia	- Fear of insects.
Eosophobia	- Fear of dawn or daylight.
Ephebiphobia	- Fear of teenagers.
Epistaxiophobia	- Fear of nosebleeds.
Epistemophobia	- Fear of knowledge.
Equinophobia	- Fear of horses.
Eremophobia	- Fear of being oneself or of lonliness.
Ereuthrophobia	- Fear of blushing.
Ergasiophobia	- 1) Fear of work or functioning. 2) Surgeon's fear of operating.

Ergophobia	- Fear of work.
Erotophobia	- Fear of sexual love or sexual questions.
Euphobia	- Fear of hearing good news.
Eurotophobia	- Fear of female genitalia.
Erythrophobia or Erytophobia or Ereuthophobia	- 1) Fear of red lights. 2) Blushing. 3) Red.
Galeophobia or Gatophobia	- Fear of cats.
Gallophobia or Galiophobia	- Fear France or French culture. (Francophobia)
Gamophobia	- Fear of marriage.
Geliophobia	- Fear of laughter.
Gelotophobia	- Fear of being laughed at.
Geniophobia	- Fear of chins.
Genophobia	- Fear of sex.
Genuphobia	- Fear of knees.
Gephyrophobia or Gephydrophobia or Gephysrophobia	- Fear of crossing bridges.
Germanophobia	- Fear of Germany or German culture.
Gerascophobia	- Fear of growing old.
Gerontophobia	- Fear of old people or of growing old.
Geumaphobia or Geumophobia	- Fear of taste.
Glossophobia	- Fear of speaking in public or of trying to speak.
Gnosiophobia	- Fear of knowledge.
Graphophobia	- Fear of writing or handwriting.

Gymnophobia - Fear of nudity.

Gynephobia
or Gynophobia - Fear of women.

Hadephobia - Fear of hell.

Hagiophobia - Fear of saints or holy things.

Hamartophobia - Fear of sinning.

Haphephobia
or Haptephobia - Fear of being touched.

Harpaxophobia - Fear of being robbed.

Hedonophobia - Fear of feeling pleasure.

Heliophobia - Fear of the sun.

Hellenologophobia - Fear of Greek terms or complex scientific terminology.

Helminthophobia - Fear of being infested with worms.

Hemophobia
or Hemaphobia
or Hematophobia - Fear of blood.

Heresyphobia
or Hereiophobia - Fear of challenges to official doctrine or of radical deviation.

Herpetophobia - Fear of reptiles or creepy, crawly things.

Heterophobia - Fear of the opposite sex. (Sexophobia)

Hexakosioihexekontahexaphobia - Fear of the number 666.

Hierophobia - Fear of priests or sacred things.

Hippophobia - Fear of horses.

Hippopotomonstrosesquipedaliophobia - Fear of long words.

Hobophobia - Fear of bums or beggars.

Hodophobia - Fear of road travel.

Hormephobia - Fear of shock.

Homichlophobia - Fear of fog.

Homilophobia	- Fear of sermons.
Hominophobia	- Fear of men.
Homophobia	- Fear of sameness, monotony or of homosexuality or of becoming homosexual.
Hoplophobia	- Fear of firearms.
Hydrargyophobia	- Fear of mercurial medicines.
Hydrophobia	- Fear of water or of rabies.
Hydrophobophobia	- Fear of rabies.
Hyelophobia or Hyalophobia	- Fear of glass.
Hygrophobia	- Fear of liquids, dampness, or moisture.
Hylephobia	- Fear of materialism or the fear of epilepsy.
Hylophobia	- Fear of forests.
Hypengyophobia or Hypegiaphobia	- Fear of responsibility.
Hypnophobia	- Fear of sleep or of being hypnotized.
Hypsiphobia	- Fear of height.
Iatrophobia	- Fear of going to the doctor or of doctors.
Ichthyophobia	- Fear of fish.
Ideophobia	- Fear of ideas.
Illyngophobia	- Fear of vertigo or feeling dizzy when looking down.
Iophobia	- Fear of poison.
Insectophobia	- Fear of insects.
Isolophobia	- Fear of solitude, being alone.
Isopterophobia	- Fear of termites, insects that eat wood.
Ithyphallophobia	- Fear of seeing, thinking about or having an erect penis.

Kainolophobia or Kainophobia	- Fear of anything new, novelty.
Kakorrhaphiophobia	- Fear of failure or defeat.
Katagelophobia	- Fear of ridicule.
Kathisophobia	- Fear of sitting down.
Katsaridaphobia	- Fear of cockroaches.
Kenophobia	- Fear of voids or empty spaces.
Keraunophobia or Ceraunophobia	- Fear of thunder and lightning. (Astraphobia, Astrapophobia)
Kinetophobia or Kinesophobia	- Fear of movement or motion.
Kleptophobia	- Fear of stealing.
Koinoniphobia	- Fear of rooms.
Kolpophobia	- Fear of genitals, particularly female.
Kopophobia	- Fear of fatigue.
Koniophobia	- Fear of dust. (Amathophobia)
Kosmikophobia	- Fear of cosmic phenomenon.
Kymophobia	- Fear of waves. (Cymophobia)
Kynophobia	- Fear of rabies.
Kyphophobia	- Fear of stooping.
Lachanophobia	- Fear of vegetables.
Laliophobia or Lalophobia	- Fear of speaking.
Leprophobia or Lepraphobia	- Fear of leprosy.
Leukophobia	- Fear of the color white.
Levophobia	- Fear of things to the left side of the body.
Ligyrophobia	- Fear of loud noises.
Lilapsophobia	- Fear of tornadoes and hurricanes.

Limnophobia - Fear of lakes.
Linonophobia - Fear of string.
Liticaphobia - Fear of lawsuits.
Lockiophobia - Fear of childbirth.
Logizomechanophobia - Fear of computers.
Logophobia - Fear of words.
Luiphobia - Fear of lues, syphillis.
Lutraphobia - Fear of otters.
Lygophobia - Fear of darkness.
Lyssophobia - Fear of rabies or of becoming mad.
Macrophobia - Fear of long waits.
Mageirocophobia - Fear of cooking.
Maieusiophobia - Fear of childbirth.
Malaxophobia - Fear of love play. (Sarmassophobia)
Maniaphobia - Fear of insanity.
Mastigophobia - Fear of punishment.
Mechanophobia - Fear of machines.
Medomalacuphobia - Fear of losing an erection.
Medorthophobia - Fear of an erect penis.
Megalophobia - Fear of large things.
Melissophobia - Fear of bees.
Melanophobia - Fear of the color black.
Melophobia - Fear or hatred of music.
Meningitophobia - Fear of brain disease.
Menophobia - Fear of menstruation.
Merinthophobia - Fear of being bound or tied up.
Metallophobia - Fear of metal.
Metathesiophobia - Fear of changes.

Meteorophobia	- Fear of meteors.
Methyphobia	- Fear of alcohol.
Metrophobia	- Fear or hatred of poetry.
Microbiophobia	- Fear of microbes. (Bacillophobia)
Microphobia	- Fear of small things.
Misophobia or Mysophobia	- Fear of being contaminated with dirt or germs.
Mnemophobia	- Fear of memories.
Molysmophobia or Molysomophobia	- Fear of dirt or contamination.
Monophobia	- Fear of solitude or being alone.
Monopathophobia	- Fear of definite disease.
Motorphobia	- Fear of automobiles.
Mottephobia	- Fear of moths.
Musophobia or Muriphobia	- Fear of mice.
Mycophobia	- Fear or aversion to mushrooms.
Mycrophobia	- Fear of small things.
Myctophobia	- Fear of darkness.
Myrmecophobia	- Fear of ants.
Mythophobia	- Fear of myths or stories or false statements.
Myxophobia	- Fear of slime. (Blennophobia)
Nebulaphobia	- Fear of fog. (Homichlophobia)
Necrophobia	- Fear of death or dead things.
Nelophobia	- Fear of glass.
Neopharmaphobia	- Fear of new drugs.
Neophobia	- Fear of anything new.
Nephophobia	- Fear of clouds.

Noctiphobia	- Fear of the night.
Nomatophobia	- Fear of names.
Nosocomephobia	- Fear of hospitals.
Nosophobia or Nosemaphobia	- Fear of becoming ill.
Nostophobia	- Fear of returning home.
Novercaphobia	- Fear of your step - mother.
Nucleomituphobia	- Fear of nuclear weapons.
Nudophobia	- Fear of nudity.
Numerophobia	- Fear of numbers.
Nyctohylophobia	- Fear of dark wooded areas or of forests at night
Nyctophobia	- Fear of the dark or of night.
Obesophobia	- Fear of gaining weight. (Pocrescophobia)
Ochlophobia	- Fear of crowds or mobs.
Ochophobia	- Fear of vehicles.
Octophobia	- Fear of the figure 8.
Odontophobia	- Fear of teeth or dental surgery.
Odynophobia or Odynephobia	- Fear of pain. (Algophobia)
Oenophobia	- Fear of wines.
Oikophobia	- Fear of home surroundings, house. (Domatophobia, Eicophobia)
Olfactophobia	- Fear of smells.
Ombrophobia	- Fear of rain or of being rained on.
Ommetaphobia or Ommatophobia	- Fear of eyes.
Omphalophobia	- Fear of belly buttons.
Oneirophobia	- Fear of dreams.
Oneirogmophobia	- Fear of wet dreams.

Onomatophobia	- Fear of hearing a certain word or of names.
Ophidiophobia	- Fear of snakes. (Snake phobia)
Ophthalmophobia	- Fear of being stared at.
Opiophobia	- Fear medical doctor's experience of prescribing needed pain medications for patients.
Optophobia	- Fear of opening one's eyes.
Ornithophobia	- Fear of birds.
Orthophobia	- Fear of property.
Osmophobia or Osphresiophobia	- Fear of smells or odors.
Ostraconophobia	- Fear of shellfish.
Ouranophobia or Uranophobia	- Fear of heaven.
Pagophobia	- Fear of ice or frost.
Panthophobia	- Fear of suffering and disease.
Panophobia or Pantophobia	- Fear of everything.
Papaphobia	- Fear of the Pope.
Papyrophobia	- Fear of paper.
Paralipophobia	- Fear of neglecting duty or responsibility.
Paraphobia	- Fear of sexual perversion.
Parasitophobia	- Fear of parasites.
Paraskavedekatriaphobia	- Fear of Friday the 13th.
Parthenophobia	- Fear of virgins or young girls.
Pathophobia	- Fear of disease.
Patroiophobia	- Fear of heredity.
Parturiphobia	- Fear of childbirth.
Peccatophobia	- Fear of sinning or imaginary crimes.

Pediculophobia	- Fear of lice.
Pediophobia	- Fear of dolls.
Pedophobia	- Fear of children.
Peladophobia	- Fear of bald people.
Pellagrophobia	- Fear of pellagra.
Peniaphobia	- Fear of poverty.
Pentheraphobia	- Fear of mother-in-law. (Novercaphobia)
Phagophobia	- Fear of swallowing or of eating or of being eaten.
Phalacrophobia	- Fear of becoming bald.
Phallophobia	- Fear of a penis, especially erect.
Pharmacophobia	- Fear of taking medicine.
Phasmophobia	- Fear of ghosts.
Phengophobia	- Fear of daylight or sunshine.
Philemaphobia or Philematophobia	- Fear of kissing.
Philophobia	- Fear of falling in love or being in love.
Philosophobia	- Fear of philosophy.
Phobophobia	- Fear of phobias.
Photoaugliaphobia	- Fear of glaring lights.
Photophobia	- Fear of light.
Phonophobia	- Fear of noises or voices or one's own voice; of telephones.
Phronemophobia	- Fear of thinking.
Phthiriophobia	- Fear of lice. (Pediculophobia)
Phthisiophobia	- Fear of tuberculosis.
Placophobia	- Fear of tombstones.
Plutophobia	- Fear of wealth.
Pluviophobia	- Fear of rain or of being rained on.

Pneumatiphobia	- Fear of spirits.
Pnigophobia or Pnigerophobia	- Fear of choking of being smothered.
Pocrescophobia	- Fear of gaining weight. (Obesophobia)
Pogonophobia	- Fear of beards.
Poliosophobia	- Fear of contracting poliomyelitis.
Politicophobia	- Fear or abnormal dislike of politicians.
Polyphobia	- Fear of many things.
Poinephobia	- Fear of punishment.
Ponophobia	- Fear of overworking or of pain.
Porphyrophobia	- Fear of the color purple.
Potamophobia	- Fear of rivers or running water.
Potophobia	- Fear of alcohol.
Pharmacophobia	- Fear of drugs.
Proctophobia	- Fear of rectums.
Prosophobia	- Fear of progress.
Psellismophobia	- Fear of stuttering.
Psychophobia	- Fear of mind.
Psychrophobia	- Fear of cold.
Pteromerhanophobia	- Fear of flying.
Pteronophobia	- Fear of being tickled by feathers.
Pupaphobia	- Fear of puppets.
Pyrexiophobia	- Fear of Fever.
Pyrophobia	- Fear of fire.
Radiophobia	- Fear of radiation, x - rays.
Ranidaphobia	- Fear of frogs.
Rectophobia	- Fear of rectum or rectal diseases.

Rhabdophobia	- Fear of being severely punished or beaten by a rod, or of being severely criticized. Also fear of magic. (wand)
Rhypophobia	- Fear of defecation.
Rhytiphobia	- Fear of getting wrinkles.
Rupophobia	- Fear of dirt.
Russophobia	- Fear of Russians.
Samhainophobia	- Fear of Halloween.
Sarmassophobia	- Fear of love play. (Malaxophobia)
Satanophobia	- Fear of Satan.
Scabiophobia	- Fear of scabies.
Scatophobia	- Fear of fecal matter.
Scelerophibia	- Fear of bad men, burglars.
Sciophobia or Sciaphobia	- Fear of shadows.
Scoleciphobia	- Fear of worms.
Scolionophobia	- fear of school.
Scopophobia or Scoptophobia	- Fear of being seen or stared at.
Scotomaphobia	- Fear of blindness in visual field.
Scotophobia	- Fear of darkness. (Achluophobia)
Scriptophobia	- Fear of writing in public.
Selachophobia	- Fear of sharks.
Selaphobia	- Fear of light flashes.
Selenophobia	- Fear of the moon.
Seplophobia	- Fear of decaying matter.
Sesquipedalophobia	- Fear of long words.
Sexophobia	- Fear of the opposite sex. (Heterophobia)
Siderodromophobia	- Fear of trains, railroads or train travel.

Siderophobia - Fear of stars.

Sinistrophobia - Fear of things to the left or left - handed.

Sinophobia - Fear of Chinese, Chinese culture.

Sitophobia or Sitiophobia - Fear of food or eating. (Cibophobia)

Snakephobia - Fear of snakes. (Ophidiophobia)

Soceraphobia - Fear of parents - in - law.

Social Phobia - Fear of being evaluated negatively in social situations.

Sociophobia - Fear of society or people in general.

Somniphobia - Fear of sleep.

Sophophobia - Fear of learning.

Soteriophobia - Fear of dependence on others.

Spacephobia - Fear of outer space.

Spectrophobia - Fear of specters or ghosts.

Spermatophobia or Spermophobia - Fear of germs.

Spheksophobia - Fear of wasps.

Stasibasiphobia or Stasiphobia - Fear of standing or walking. (Ambulophobia)

Staurophobia - Fear of crosses or the crucifix.

Stenophobia - Fear of narrow things or places.

Stygiophobia or Stigiophobia - Fear of hell.

Suriphobia - Fear of mice.

Symbolophobia - Fear of symbolism.

Symmetrophobia - Fear of symmetry.

Syngenesophobia - Fear of relatives.

Syphilophobia - Fear of syphilis.

Tachophobia	- Fear of speed.
Taeniophobia or Teniophobia	- Fear of tapeworms.
Taphephobia or Taphophobia	- Fear of being buried alive or of cemeteries.
Tapinophobia	- Fear of being contagious.
Taurophobia	- Fear of bulls.
Technophobia	- Fear of technology.
Teleophobia	- 1) Fear of definite plans. 2) Religious ceremony.
Telephonophobia	- Fear of telephones.
Teratophobia	- Fear of bearing a deformed child or fear of monsters or deformed people.
Testophobia	- Fear of taking tests.
Tetanophobia	- Fear of lockjaw, tetanus.
Teutophobia	- Fear of German or German things.
Textophobia	- Fear of certain fabrics.
Thaasophobia	- Fear of sitting.
Thalassophobia	- Fear of the sea.
Thanatophobia or Thantophobia	- Fear of death or dying.
Theatrophobia	- Fear of theatres.
Theologicophobia	- Fear of theology.
Theophobia	- Fear of gods or religion.
Thermophobia	- Fear of heat.
Tocophobia	- Fear of pregnancy or childbirth.
Tomophobia	- Fear of surgical operations.
Tonitrophobia	- Fear of thunder.

Topophobia	- Fear of certain places or situations, such as stage fright.
Toxiphobia or Toxophobia or Toxicophobia	- Fear of poison or of being accidently poisoned.
Traumatophobia	- Fear of injury.
Tremophobia	- Fear of trembling.
Trichinophobia	- Fear of trichinosis.
Trichopathophobia or Trichophobia	- Fear of hair. (Chaetophobia, Hypertrichophobia)
Triskaidekaphobia	- Fear of the number 13.
Tropophobia	- Fear of moving or making changes.
Trypanophobia	- Fear of injections.
Tuberculophobia	- Fear of tuberculosis.
Tyrannophobia	- Fear of tyrants.
Vaccinophobia	- Fear of vaccination.
Venustraphobia	- Fear of beautiful women.
Verbophobia	- Fear of words.
Verminophobia	- Fear of germs.
Vestiphobia	- Fear of clothing.
Virginitiphobia	- Fear of rape.
Vitricophobia	- Fear of step - father.
Xanthophobia	- Fear of the color yellow or the word yellow.
Xenoglossophobia	- Fear of foreign languages.
Xenophobia	- Fear of strangers or foreigners.
Xerophobia	- Fear of dryness.
Xylophobia	- 1) Fear of wooden objects. 2) Forests.

Xyrophobia	- Fear of razors.
Zelophobia	- Fear of jealousy.
Zeusophobia	- Fear of God or gods.
Zemmiphobia	- Fear of the great mole rat.
Zoophobia	- Fear of animals.

DON'T ACCEPT MR. FEAR! HE HAS THE ABILITY TO TAKE YOU AWAY FROM WHERE YOU COULD HAVE WON! THERE IS MORE WISDOM IN FAILURE!

4. YOU MUST BE A CHAMPION

Champion: The winner of a sporting contest or other competition. A person who argues or fight for a cause or another person according to Oxford English dictionary. To me a CHAMPION is he who doesn't see difficulties or excuses or is afraid of challenging a challenge that is challenging him to get the trophy at the end of the championship.

A CHAMPION is a celebrity. People celebrate you because you are a CHAMPION.

A CHAMPION is a fellow that has a record.

A CHAMPION is a star.

A CHAMPION brings celebrations to the minds of his fans after every event.

A CHAMPION is discussed even by people he doesn't know or hasn't met.

A CHAMPION'S name is relied on to make a brand of product move in the market.

A CHAMPION gets a lot of gifts because he wins and puts celebration on people's minds.

A CHAMPION is a go getter.

A CHAMPION is a God for his fans.

A CHAMPION fights for others to live.

A CHAMPION makes the story of his life a book for people to learn from.

A CHAMPION is always the last man standing. If you don't stand out, you can't be outstanding.

A CHAMPION could is a hero.

A CHAMPION is (himself because what he did that made him A CHAMPION could be an example for others to follow.

"A CHAMPION is the best of the best. I hated every minute of training, but I said, 'Don't quit. Suffer now and live the rest of your life as A CHAMPION."

—Muhammad Ali

"To be A CHAMPION, you have to see the big picture. It's not about winning and losing. It's about hard work and about thriving on a challenge every day. It's about embracing the pain that you experience at the end of a race. People think too hard and are afraid of a certain challenge."

—Summer Sanders

"Winning is great, sure, but if you are really going to do something in life, the secret is learning how to lose. Nobody goes undefeated all the time. If you can pick up after a crushing defeat, and go on to win again, you are going to be A CHAMPION someday."

—Wilma Rudolph

"The last three or four reps is what makes the muscle grow. This area of pain divides the Champion from someone else who is not a champion. That's what most people lack, having the guts to go on and just say they'll go through the pain no matter what happens."

—Arnold Schwarzenegger

"CHAMPIONS are not the ones who always win races - champions are the ones who get out there and try. And try harder the next time. And even harder the next time. 'Champion' is a state of mind. They are devoted. They compete to best themselves as much if not more than they compete to best others. Champions are not just athletes."

—Simon Sinek

"A CHAMPION is someone who gets up when he can't."

—Jack Dempsey

"There's always the motivation of wanting to win. Everybody has that. But A CHAMPION needs, in his attitude, a motivation above and beyond winning."

—Pat Riley

5. DON'T GIVE A REASON! LOOK FOR A WAY

"He that is good for making excuses is seldom good for anything else."

— Benjamin Franklin

In life, the only reason why man gives reasons is Mr. Failure. Mr. Failure gives you excuses for why he was unable to do something. He will give you reasons for why he failed. He will give you reasons that will make a thing not work. Mr. Failure does not look for a way but is always looking for reasons. His reasons are always flimsy. Mr. Failure can't tell you that he has a way, but, rather, he would tell you reasons for why it was so. You come into this world for a purpose. Have you fulfilled the purpose you came for? Mr. Failure leaves the purpose he came for and is looking for one thing. He forgets that it was still that same thing that makes people die. We are discussing the excuses that Mr. Failure often gives, in order to be pitied.

When you die, know it that this one purpose will take you to a place to see someone - a person or an entity, whatever it may be - and you will be judged for that one purpose. Someone said "If not for one thing I would have, if not, because of one thing, they wouldn't catch me says who? If not one thing I would have given her that stuff If not one thing I would have." Now check in all the statements of "one thing" from Mr. Failure if you see "IF and WOULD" in the statements. "IF" means request or begging. Mr. Failure likes begging and takes on all conditions imposed on him because he has no other option.

If you find yourself begging it means that you have already failed and will abide by any condition given therein. For instance, a woman needs $2000 USD for her son's hospital bill and the doctor tells her, "If the money isn't brought, I won't treat your son." The son is on the verge of death. She runs to a friend because her husband is no more. When she met with her friend, asking for money, the man insists that she must give in before he releases the money for her. This woman is between the devil and the deep blue sea. If she had any other way to get money, she could have. But now, she has no option but to give in to the man and collect the cash even if she swore not to do such a thing in her life.

Why does she give in? She gives in because she fails. This happened although she knew would regret it. But, there is always wisdom in failure. From that moment, if she did not save money till then, she would learn to save by force. She would learn to fix herself by doing something she wasn't doing. The logic behind this is that when we give excuses, things are spoiled. If this woman had given an excuse when she was given an option, her son would have died. Although it wasn't pleasing or advisable for a married woman to dance to such kind of a bit!

Did you notice that it was only a small thing that spoiled one thing? That small thing exposes everything that brought about the small excuse. What is the small thing? I believe everyone knows (Mrs. Excuse the wife of Mr. Failure). If you ask the woman for the reason behind what she did, she would give you a fine excuse saying that she doesn't want her son to die? Yes Mrs. Excuse looks so beautiful elegant and charming so pleasing to hear anytime.

Don't give excuses for why you didn't get results. Instead, look for a way because there is always one. Put in more effort and remove excuses because excuses give birth to a reason for why it was so. It is the same excuse that brought about one thing that you did. Remember, complains doesn't solve any issue. Rather, it makes the issue worse. When you complain, it means you are giving excuses instead of finding a way. Check it out, the way is always there. But because you can't or you were lazy to find it, and you bend to complaints. When you complain, so many suggestions come and if they come, it must definitely seem like a way out to you. But, not all of them are to be accepted if you bend down. Ask yourself, how long will it take to fish out the way out from the numerous suggestions? What if it's too late for the main purpose? I want you to know that in every situation, there is a perfect consultant to consult!

As humans, we have ways of doing things. That is why we are said to be expressing images of God. Everybody created by God has his own style. You should ask: What is my style? Good for you to ask now, for your own style is in you. Remember, it's the YOU in YOU that makes you who you are. That you in you is your style. What will make you not discover the you in you is when you are not satisfied with yourself. Then, it results in faking who you are. Faking, here, is used in the sense to convey that you will be trying to be who you are not - that is to say, trying to be another person. In the process, you wind up leaving behind who you are, and it tends to be forgotten that there are no two same people in this world. Someone may see another person that looks like you, but that doesn't make the person to be a second you! That is "NO" in capital letters. If he or she likes you, let them bear your name and have all the uniqueness with you. Remember, you are only one you. This should always be in your consciousness every day.

When you complain to Musa and Mary they will give you their own styles. Now who will make use of your style? Yes, you should be the one to answer that question because if you make use of their styles, what will happen to yours? It will mean that there is no you. Everybody has his or her own uniqueness.

Learning from someone doesn't mean that you should use all his or her styles. When a teacher teaches you something, he or she gives you an assignment. He didn't give you assignment because he wanted you to solve it fully from his perspective or style. He expects you to add your style by looking beyond what he taught you. No teacher will want you to give him or her verbatim of what is in your notebook or textbook as the answer for his or her assignment.

He would for love you to do some research in order to bring more of your style. The whole world is waiting for your style. Don't forget that your own style is highly necessary because you are the only one person that is you, in this world. That makes your style overly unique. Research implies digging deep in order to get more answers or solutions. Some text books written by lecturers were assignments given to their students. The students were forced to put in their own styles in order to pass. In other words, as the students put in their own styles by doing research for more knowledge on the theme, they were making their styles known to the lecturer and the Lecturer used their styles to publish his textbook. This is to tell you that your style or your way is money in itself. It is worth more than billions if only you find your style and no reasons why it wouldn't be this way. Keep it in the back of your mind that the whole world is waiting for your style because your style is what they need to change things in this world. Reject fear and embrace courage. Don't be lazy in bringing out your style. Laziness is what brings about giving reasons for why you are not able to deliver.

Remember, your style is like gold and if only you dig deep, you can get it. Take a look at these people:

I was raped at the age of '9'

—Oprah Winfrey.

I didn't even complete my university education

—Bill Gates

I in my childhood days (stitched shoes)

—Abraham Lincoln

I struggled academically throughout my elementary school

—Dr. Ben Carson.

I used to serve tea at a shop to support my football training

—Lionel Messi

I used to sleep on the floor in friends rooms returning coke bottles for food money and getting a weekly free meal at a local temple

—Steve Jobs.

My teacher used to call me a failure

—Tony Blair

I want you to know that your style is needed most in the world. Tell us that your style may be someone may try it. It may work for him and it means that you just saved a soul. Life is not all about what you could do so far, it's all about what you can do, so never give up! The last step shows you how best you can run a race.

"The only thing standing between you and your goal is the bullshit story you keep telling yourself as to why you can't achieve it."

—Jordan Belfort

"No matter how old you are now. You are never too young or too old for success or going after what you want."

—Pablo

Here's a short list of people who accomplished great things at different ages

1. Helen Keller, at 19 months was diagnosed as deaf and blind. But that didn't stop her. She was the first deaf and blind person to earn a Bachelor of Arts degree.
2. Mozart was already competent on keyboard and violin and composed from the age of 5.
3. Shirley Temple was 6 when she became a movie star on "Bright Eyes."
4. Anne Frank was 12 when she wrote the diary of Anne Frank.
5. Magnus Carlsen became a chess Grandmaster at 13.
6. Nadia Comăneci was a gymnast from Romania that scored a perfect 10.0 seven times and won three gold medals at the Olympics at 14.
7. Tenzin Gyatso was formally recognized as the 14th Dalai Lama in November 1950, at 15.
8. Pele, a soccer superstar, was 17 when he won the world cup in 1958 with Brazil.
9. Elvis was a superstar by the time he was 19.
10. John Lennon was 20 and Paul Mcartney was 18 when the Beatles had their first concert in 1961.
11. Jesse Owens was 22 when he won 4 gold medals in Berlin 1936.
12. Beethoven was a piano virtuoso by the time he was 23.

13. Isaac Newton wrote Philosophiæ Naturalis Principia Mathematica at 24.
14. Roger Bannister was 25 when he broke the 4 minute mile record.
15. Albert Einstein was 26 when he wrote the theory of relativity.
16. Lance E. Armstrong was 27 when he won the tour de France.
17. Michelangelo created two of the greatest sculptures "David" and "Pieta" by the time he was 28.
18. Alexander the Great, by 29, had created one of the largest empires of the ancient world.
19. J.K. Rowling was 30 when she finished the first manuscript of Harry Potter.
20. Amelia Earhart was 31 when she became the first woman to fly solo across the Atlantic Ocean
21. Oprah was 32 when she started her talk show, which became the highest-rated program of its kind
22. Edmund Hillary was 33 when he became the first man to climb Mount Everest.
23. Martin Luther King Jr. was 34 when he wrote the speech "I Have a Dream".
24. Marie Curie was 35 when she was nominated for a Nobel Prize in Physics
25. The Wright brothers, Orville (32) and Wilbur (36) invented and built the world's first successful airplane and making the first controlled, powered and sustained heavier-than-air human flight.
26. Vincent Van Gogh was 37 when he died virtually unknown, yet his paintings today are worth millions.
27. Neil Armstrong was 38 when he became the first man to set foot on the moon.
28. Mark Twain was 40 when he wrote "The Adventures of Tom Sawyer", and 49 when he wrote "Adventures of Huckleberry Finn".
29. Christopher Columbus was 41 when he discovered the Americas.

30. Rosa Parks was 42 when she refused to obey the bus driver's order to give up her seat to make room for a white passenger.
31. John F. Kennedy was 43 when he became President of the United States.
32. Henry Ford Was 45 when the Ford T came out.
33. Suzanne Collins was 46 when she wrote "The Hunger Games".
34. Charles Darwin was 50 when his book On the Origin of Species came out.
35. Leonardo Da Vinci was 51 when he painted the Mona Lisa.
36. Abraham Lincoln was 52 when he became the President of the United States.
37. Ray Kroc Was 53 when he bought the McDonalds Franchise and took it to unprecedented levels.
38. Dr. Seuss was 54 when he wrote "The Cat in the Hat".
39. Chesley "Sully" Sullenberger III was 57 when he successfully ditched US Airways Flight 1549 in the Hudson River in 2009. All 155 passengers aboard the aircraft survived.
40. Colonel Harland Sanders was 61 when he started the KFC Franchise.
41. J.R.R Tolkien was 62 when the Lord of the Ring books came out.
42. Ronald Reagan was 69 when he became the President of the US.
43. Jack Lalane at age 70 handcuffed, shackled, towed 70 rowboats.
44. Nelson Mandela was 76 when he became President".

6. THE HAND THAT IS ON TOP (A GIVER)

A giver is someone who devotes himself completely. There are no greater givers than those who give themselves. A good person is a person who is good to other people. A giver is a person who makes a gift of property. A giver is a person who makes a gift of property, bestowal, conferrer, donor, presenter.

Benefactor is a person who helps people or institutions (especially with financial help).

Abnegator is one who gives up or relinquishes or renounces something.

Almsgiver is a person who gives alms

An Indian giver is an offensive term for someone who asks you to return a present he has given you.

An altruist or philanthropist is someone who makes charitable donations intended to increase human well-being.

A settlor or trustor (is a person who creates a trust by giving real or personal property in trust to a trustee for the benefit of a beneficiary. A person who gives such property is said to settle it on the trustee.

A contributor and subscriber is someone who contributes (or promises to contribute) a sum of money.

A subsidizer is someone who assists or supports by giving a subsidy.

A tipper is a person who leaves a tip; "a generous tipper"

The hand that is on top is always blessed. For you to be called a blessing, your hand must be on top. The hand that is on top is always enriched to reach out. The hand that is on top doesn't lack anything. Givers never lack. It is recorded in the Holy Scriptures 'that blessed is the hand that gives than the one that takes'. People are always looking for success. The secret of success is in giving because when you stop giving, you start lacking. Be conscious of giving. Let your mentality everyday be 'who shall I bless today with my giving?' When you give, you put a smile on somebody's face. There is a special joy when giving makes someone smile. Don't give because you want men to notice you but give because that given needs to be done. Don't give for people to give you glory but give for God to be glorified. Don't give because you want to show yourself off but give because there is no other one that God could use for that purpose and at that moment, beside you. Don't give in mockery because there is no blessing attached to it. Don't announce to your left hand that you gave with your right hand because when you do that, you are seeking glory just for yourself and there is no blessing attached to it. Your giving creates a chance for a plenteous replacement. If nothing did go out, nothing will come in to replace it.

Note: There is no place that is empty in life. If you remove water from a vessel, it is not because there is air in the vessel. This means that everything that is taken out should be replacement whether spiritual or physical.

Look at his short story below: a poor man waited at the bus stand to board a bus, he had Rs. 2000 with him. As he enter, he saw a mad man who begged him for some money. He pushed the mad man away and had been praying all month to God to bless him financially. Now he pushed the mad man away and entered the bus. However, immediately the poor man got home and saw his spiritual leader and explained everything that happened to the spiritual leader and the spiritual leader told him that the mad man was an angel that was sent to bless him and make him wealthy. He went back to look for the mad man and give him money. Unfortunately for him, when he got back, he couldn't find the mad man again.

DON'T MISS OUT ON THE OPPURTUNITY FOR GIVING. YOU'RE THE PROPERITY IN YOUR BLESSING LIES IN GIVING.

7. CHANGE YOUR MIND SET

Ignorance is cheap. If you think education is costly try ignorance because as far as I know, ignorance is cheap. It cost nothing to be ignorant. A fool at 40 is a fool forever because he doesn't know that he doesn't know is a big fool. A fool jumps into conclusions because he doesn't think before he talks. He always talks before he thinks. A wise man thinks before he talks and never talks without listening.

Too much education makes you look stupid, do you know? Don't misconstrue me. First, see my opinion before you condemn me. You might think that I started by saying that education is good. Now, I am saying that it makes someone look stupid. I didn't say that studying is not good but to make it in life, what you need is to change your mind-set, or (the way you see things about life. In college, your lecturer only lectures or teaches you how to work and earn money in life, but they don't teach you how to make money and be great. They teach you how to MANAGE in life instead of DIRECTING. Managing and directing are different words. Don't forget that earning money and making money is not same thing. You must keep that in mind. Great men do the same thing that others do, but in a different way. The two daddies: Rich daddy and Poor daddy: the difference in them is their MINDSET. Rich daddy lives in optimism because of his MINDSET. But poor daddy lives in criticism and that is his mentality. Everybody that made it in LIFE is either called a fraudster. People call his earning blood money. We have been using the currency notes there is no place on the note that was painted with blood. To the Poor daddy, anybody that has a luxurious car is not genuine, anybody that built a good house is not genuine and that is because of the condition of his state of mind. He spends time looking into other people's matters instead of utilizing his time and effort to bring forth ideas that will change the world. The Rich Daddy thinks and always brings out ideas. He spends less time sleeping and discussing people. His brains are working 24 hours a day. He does not struggle, rather, he spends time - and when I say time - I mean quality time, in thinking. He doesn't rest until he thinks of new ways of changing others' lives. The Poor Daddy is always filled with illusions. Let's go back to why I said to you that the more education or otherwise more studies you indulge in, the more you became stupid.

When I bend down, I see that the number of men and women that made headway or left a mark on the world, actually never went to school. It was the conditioning of their mind sets that put them in a place to that pick in life. It was the same state of mind that lead them to come up with numerous ideas and today, they are all world class. When you are over-educated, what you think of is only about how to work for other people. You don't think of invention. Check it all out around you. 90% of the graduates around you are looking for jobs. They sleep and wakeup, meditating on how much a company can pay them if they succeed in an interview. Funny! I realized that 90% of the people went to school end up being working class people. Making it in life doesn't lie on what you were thought of at school. It lies on your MINDSET that propels you to make use of the idea you had because one idea can change the whole world.

Obinna and Ogan were schoolmates studying the same course in college. Both of them had a different mentality. Obinna is currently studying to work in Samsung but Ogan is only thinking of how to buy Samsung. That is Ogan's MINDSET. But the question you will ask is, how will he buy the company? We know that Samsung is worth billions of dollars. YOU have to first buy it with your mind before anything else. As years went by, Ogan came up with an idea that caused the company's value to increase so much, even making the company among the top three in the world. He earned a stake and became one of the decision-makers in the board of directors as a result of his huge stake in the company. The people that study a lot end up working and people that have ideas explode!

If you tell a poor mind that you want to buy an aircraft, he would first laugh asking you if you have a fever. Why does he laugh? Because he knows that you don't have the money to buy a car, much less even talk of an aircraft. The reason behind his asking and laughing is because a poor mind thinks of impossibilities. He never sees possibility in anything. His mind is filled with impossibilities and nothing more. That was why I said that he didn't know that he is a big fool. The poor mind is a fool. It is also full of witchcraft in his mind. He doesn't know. This is why I asked: "Who are your friends?" Tell me your friends and I can tell you what you can do. Are they those that see only impossibilities? Do they say "it doesn't work"? If they do, decamp fast! They have a different MINDSET. If you don't decamp, two options are available... Either they affect you or you affect them. But it will be crazy and bad if they are the ones that affected you. The worse thing that can happen to someone who is going somewhere is to sit down on a discussion with someone who is going nowhere, because you will definitely miss your flight. If you want to miss your flight in life, engage in a discussion with someone who is going nowhere. Be wise. Wisdom is divine. Don't learn from the mistake you will make, learn from the others' mistakes as well. You can't live to make all the mistakes. Your success is not based on how much education you have, but on your MINDSET. Your mind has the power to carry the whole world. Begin to cook beautiful things in your mind learn how to develop it with good thought and achievements. Look at the richest in the world. They never went to school but now have ability to pay PhD holders as their staff members in their companies! If I may ask, how many professors are among the world's richest? Your MINDSET is what you need to change for the better. Look out for that thing that makes you who you are and find it.

How you can Change Your Mind Set

When you approach a challenge, there is always a voice that says: "Are you sure you can do it? What if you fail in the process? Don't you think people might call you a failure? What if People will laugh at you for thinking you had talent?" Trying is the answer. If you don't try, you can't protect yourself and keep your dignity.

If you meet a setback or a bigger challenge, the voice might say, "This would have been a snap if you really had talent! I told you it was a risk. Now you've shown the world how limited you are. It's not too late to back out, make excuses, and try to regain your dignity!" Remember, there is always a way. That voice itself is the setback you are seeing at that moment. If there is criticism, you might hear the voice saying to you, "It's not my fault. It was something or someone else's fault!" You might feel like you are getting angry at the person who is giving you feedback. "Who do they think they are?" But you might be hearing them say "I'm really disappointed in you. I thought you were capable of it, but I see you're not." Don't listen to that voice. It's a setback. Remember, you have a choice always.

How you understand challenges and criticism is your choice. You can understand them in a fixed mindset. You can interpret them as signs that you need to ramp up your strategies and efforts and expand your abilities. It's your choice. As you face challenges and criticism, listen to the VOICE that says you can do it. As you approach a challenge, if the setback says "Are you really sure you can do it? Maybe you don't have what it takes." ALWAYS listen to the voice that answers, "I'm sure I can do it, I think it takes only my time and effort." If the little voice asks you what if you fail, have the boldness to answer "Most successful people had failures along the way!" Trying gives you the result you are waiting for… Ask Thomas Edison! Always, do not listen to the little voice that says "It's not my fault. It was something or someone else's fault." Remember, if you don't take responsibility, you can't fix it. However, have the "I can do mentality." Take up the challenge with your whole heart. Learn from the mistakes you made. Listen to the criticism and act on it as it is now in your hands. Your MINDSET is what put you in that place you are today. THINK STRAIGHT TODAY.

8. SEE THROUGH MY VIEW

SEE

1. Perceive with the eyes; discern visually. "In the distance she could see the blue sea."

   Synonyms: discern, perceive, glimpse, catch/get a glimpse of, spot, notice, catch, sight of, sight; Make out, pick out, spy, distinguish, identify, recognize, detect, note, mark; Informal clap/lay/set eyes on, clock; Literary behold, descry, espy

   Synonyms: watch, look at, view, observe, and catch

2. Discern or deduce after reflection or from information; understand. "I can't see any other way to treat it".

   Synonyms: understand, grasp, comprehend, follow, take in, realize, appreciate, recognize, work out, get the drift of, make out, conceive, perceive, fathom (out), become cognizant of; informal get, latch on to, cotton on to, catch on to, tumble to, figure out, get the hang of, get a fix on, get one's head round/around, get the message, get the picture;

   Synonyms: foresee, predict, forecast, prophesy, prognosticate, anticipate, envisage, envision, picture, visualize;

THROUGH

Moving in one side and out of the other side of (an opening, channel, or location). "Stepping boldly through the doorway"

Synonyms: into and out of, to the other/far side of, from one side of...to the other, from end to end of, between, past, by, down, along, across, by way of,

View

The ability to see something or to be seen from a particular place.

"The end of the tunnel came into view"

Synonyms: sight, perspective, field of vision, range of vision, vision, visibility, eyeshot

Seeing Through Someone's View is to Come to One's Own Side of View to Clear a Doubt of Belief

The only reason why some people criticize each other's activity is because of a lack of understanding. If something happens, don't jump into conclusions. Try and see it from both sides. Kumar might be seeing something bad and Rakish tells you that this thing Kumar is condemning, is useful. That it is bad in the sight of Kumar doesn't make it totally bad, because someone is making use of it somewhere else. Many said that a frog is not a good meat but some countries eat it. Some doctors said if one takes a mango and a soft drink it will kill them. But I tried it I am still writing today. Many things are told to be an abomination is not necessarily so. One man's food is another man's poison.

How can you criticize something when you are not using it? First check the negative and positive side of it. Even if you finished checking both and come to the conclusion that you are right in your point of view, that you were right doesn't make you condemn or further your criticism because the other side of people you were against have their reasons backing them. Hold your view and diplomatically see if they can see your view.

Views are to be reviewed to know the proper shape. If views are not reviewed, criticism will abound enough to lead to war. For instance, in some part of the world men sleep with their daughters and some, women sleep with their sons. Some sleep with their sisters in the name of culture. To you, this may seem inappropriate, or nonsense. What exactly is nonsense here? Some street boys get married to their sisters. What do you have to say about this? Some boys drag their mothers with their fathers because if their father couldn't respect himself by having their mother alone and he is dragging the sister with the boy, the boy has no option than to move to the mother. Now you are seeing these things as wrong, as an abomination. The only thing that makes what they are doing bad as far as I am concerned, is religion. But scientifically and naturally man is an animal. The difference between man and other animals is just the higher brain man has.

When I was growing up during, when we went to church, we saw a lady wearing trousers. We said she was a harlot. In fact, you dare not come to church wearing it! These days man has travelled and returns home seeing the world through viewpoints of others. It made me understand that a woman in trousers doesn't make her bad! If a guy grooms his hair well, we say, why did that brother perm his hair he looks like a woman!

I was blind to some issues until I travelled to many countries. There are some men whose hair is longer than the women's, in my home country. What I am trying to make you understand is that dressing is about culture. When you see someone wearing something, it doesn't concern you. Have you seen women half-naked, some fully naked, in the name of fashion? What do you have to say about this? When you were born, were you born with any clothes? No matter how rich you may claim to be, your wife gives birth to a child that comes to the world naked.

When you tell someone that what he is doing is not good, first make him understand your reasons explaining your point of view. If they see it and choose to remain with their own viewpoint, leave them, because man has the right to make choices. Don't say that because he refuses to come to your side, his views are rubbish. There is no way to measure good and bad except for the laws of GOD and the laws of the land. What if they don't know the laws of God and the laws of the land?

If you want to make someone see and believe that N could be seen as Z from another view, you should first know that N stands for (nature) and make him understand what nature is, its disadvantages and give him reasons why he should believe you. Definitely, he can see things from your viewpoint.

Point B: => Z Z = Zebra

For you to see this diagram as Z, you have simply move to point B. For you to see this as N, you must come to point A. This is to show you that every issue has many viewpoints. It depends on the angle that you are seeing it from. That will make you condemn or criticize it. Don't forget that the same diagram that you are busy trying to call N is being called Z for someone else. When you criticize, give reasons and don't condemn, because your reasons are not enough until you are can convince the other.

Look at this case study. Christians claims that they bury their dead because they believe that every human being was made from dust therefore must go back to the soil. Muslims bury their dead too. There is no need to allow a person to stay more than a day before burial even if you are the president of the country. The way one is buried is the same for every other. To the Buddhists and Hindus, cremation is the way. You might ask why some people waste soil meant to cultivate food and other things? Whether you like it or not, all of them in their practices have their viewpoints.

9. POWER OF WORDS

Don't joke about words, because they are powerful. Any word that comes out of your mouth has weight. When you joke, don't forget that it's like joking with a blade. You know that it's as sharp as anything. It can cut. Be positive whenever you joke, too, don't joke against words. Don't make statements that are carless because they produce results. That is why you must say only what you mean. Be careful in your choice of words. The spirit gives you whatever you say and not what you mean. In the realm of the spirit you have whatever you say, whether or not you mean it. The Bible records in the Book of Mark 11:23: "You shall have anything, I mean, whatsoever you say. Remember it never said that you shall have whatever you mean, but whatever you say.

Words are powerful. If God could use words and this world is like this and he said we will do greater things beyond what he did when He was on earth. It was by the power of the Holy Ghost. Who is this Holy Ghost? It is God's spirit. He promised that after he leaves, he would send the holy to come and dwell richly in us. Since he is God and He did all these and he is telling us that we are gods, we can do the same. If he uses words to create, that means we can use words and create things too. From today, start practicing using nice words for yourself. If anyone tells you bad words tell him that it's not consistent with what God says you are. It is as simple as the alphabet. Change the way you talk today and talk right, because talking right has the ability to bring forth the turnaround you have been waiting for all this while. THE POWER OF WORDS!

10. ANGER

Anger is not a good commodity to keep. When you are angry the peace in you runs away. Anger makes enemies. Anger ignites wars, fights and catastrophe. Anger can put you in a state of regret anytime, any day. Anger makes you look ugly at the moment of expression. Anger brings out the beast in you. Anger puts you in a different state by influencing your thought at that moment, so that you can defeat your opponent. Anger is destructive. When you are angry, you can do stupid things. Anger reduces your lifespan. Anger makes you lose charge of your mind. When you are angry everything that comes in your mind is negative. Don't make decision when you are angry. Don't forget that decisions made in anger calls for regret later on.

No one doubts the need our bodies have for nourishment to keep them healthy. Our minds need nourishment too, to keep functioning well. Our bodies starve when nourishment is not available, and that renders us incapacitated. So too, when minds are blocked from nourishment, they starve and stop functioning.

The nourishment our mind needs is information and knowledge stored and used in a right and peaceful atmosphere leading to healthy behavior. It is a physiological reality that we are affected by turbulence of anger.

11. A SET TIME

A set time, or as I call it is effort input divided by time plus or minus God's final say, and that greater than or equals the distance between your dream and success.

Effort Input = God's final say the distance between dream and success = A set time!!!

E.I GFS distance between the dream and success = A.S.T

God is the master planner or the chief programmer. The master of the whole universe, the maker of the earth, the only one that never comes late. He does his things at the right time and at a set time. There is the always a set time. The question is, how do you know the set time if the master (has not spoken or given you an appointment? It is when you book an appointment with him that you will have a set time, as otherwise, you have to do your own thing, set your own time and get your own result. I will tell you how to book an appointment with Him so you will have a set time. I will tell you how to book an appointment with God. Any exam taken without the examination council doesn't have a certificate. Correct? Someone can decide to take exams for himself just to know his or her ability towards the main exams. It is only God who can give you an appointment with authenticity.

A set time is beyond what humans can fathom. Men always put their thought first without remembering that it is only God who has the final say. His final say is the set time.

Let's assume that you have a bridge in your village and the bridge is due to be reconstructed. It has not been reconstructed. Because of this, to enter your village, you will have to go roundabout, and that costs you time. If the members of the house agree without the president signing the contract, you know that it can never be done. Why? He has the final say. It is when he signs the document that you can build the bridge. You must put effort and as you put that effort by either writing to the government or the people that matter, you have to wait for their response first and that wait is time. When they respond and agree, it doesn't mean it's done. The bridge must be constructed. Then there is a conclusion on the matter.

The holy book recorded that JESUS was going about doing good. He was doing all sorts of wonders, healing the sick and raising the dead. The holy book records that He came from heaven to earth to show us the way and carry our sins in order to reconcile us with God. When it was *A set time* for Jesus to be betrayed, He was betrayed by JUDAS Iscariot. Judas had stayed a long time with him since the Jews wanted to kill Jesus, yet he couldn't betray Him because it was not A set time! Not only did Judas do what he did but the Jews couldn't have captured Him if not because it was A set time. Were they able to do to Him anything even when He was teaching the professors? What about when he was scattering and pursing men from the church to make it a market place?

The holy book recorded that Mr. Death couldn't hold him captive even in the grave He is still Lord. Mr. Death couldn't hold Him captive because it wasn't A set time for him to leave that environment. When He died, when the enemies succeeded in killing Him, before that, He had already told them that if they destroyed this house, He would build it is just in three (days. Those folks thought He was talking about the church. They did not know that He was talking in parables that He would rise again in just three days. Even when he told them that He would rise on the third day, they challenged him, forgetting that he is God. When the soldiers succeeded in carrying a million kilograms' stone and put it on top of his grave, what happened? Jesus rose. But why didn't Jesus rise on the first day or the second? It was simply because it wasn't A set time. God's final say was on the third day and on that day at the right hour, He rose from the grave. Why didn't the soldiers hold Him the way they were holding Him before? Because it was a set time. Imagine a soldier on duty. If I was their commander I would sack them. But, how could he, the commander, kill them when he was asleep with them all? A set time.

Can you avoid A set time? Nobody can. The third day was God's approved date. He journeyed from the first day, second day to the last day which implies a distance. He ascended to heaven. Just give your life to Christ by seeing Jesus as your personal Lord and Savior. Then, you will be among us. Some fools may say that the announcement of His coming is too much and has been a long time since it's been said. The reason why he's not come yet is because He is waiting for a set time. At that set time we will see Him in glory. Whatever you face in life has an expiry date and that is a set time too.

You complain that you don't have money. Look away and start relishing every moment in life. Everything about life happens in its own time - *A* set time.

A time to born and a time to die, A time to laugh and a time to be sad, A time to jubilate and a time to mourn, A time to sleep and a time to walk, A time to come and a time to go and A time to love and a time to hate.

The holy book recorded that when the cloud is full of rain, it must empty itself. When will it empty itself? At the set time. Learn to relax your mind in the word of God. Some will say: "I prayed to God. He answered me!" Remember, He didn't answer you because yours prayers were sweet but because in his programmes in your life, it was the set time for Him to answer that prayer. What about he whose prayer was not answered? Does it mean that God hates them? The holy book recorded that before I was born He knew me and knows what I will become. He knew from my beginning to my end.

A set time is like a bomb. Does a time bomb explode before the time? No. if you set the time for 1.5 hours for the bomb to explode and you are targeting to kill your enemies who are coming after you. The question is, if those enemies pass the bridge before that time ends, will the bomb explode? No. Will the time bomb explode because it sees your enemies? No. The time bomb doesn't know you or your enemies. It doesn't know that you were the one that fixed it or who your enemy is. At the set time, it has to explode.

A woman is pregnant and at the set time, she delivers. When is the set time? Some will say that she ought to deliver after nine (months. But what if she delivers after the ninth month? Will you say that it is not a baby? What if she delivers before the ninth month? Will you say it's not a baby? The moment she delivers is A set time.

I didn't forget Joseph in the holy book when he spoke about his dream to his brothers. They bowed before him. Even though the time for the act had not yet come, the siblings tried to stop that from happening by selling him. God has already designed your programme in life. He has prepared a way for you to go. This is why God preserved Joseph till the set time. When the set time came, he became that Royal in the kingdom. It was necessary for his brothers to bow before him.

You are struggling now because you think you can make it by your own power. But, that doesn't mean that you shouldn't put in effort, because God said that He would crown your effort with success, but at *A set time.* You may be down and feel like God had somehow forgotten you, but remember, God has proven, time and time again. Mark the words PROVEN TIME. This replaces the words A set time. God's proven time is A set time.

When you make it in life, give God the glory for it. When you travel through life with struggles and pain, and somehow make it, remember, you were and are never alone. You are always with someone you don't see. Wait and travel through the night with sweet dreams. Don't remember it as a night. When morning comes, you will not remember that you did sleep at night. Wait for the set time!

God is time and He is the master planner, and the chief programmer of all programs. All the passwords are in His hands. If He has the passwords of all your programs it means that He is the software and you are the user. If you are on a computer system now and it is booting up, keep in mind that you must wait for the programs to round up and wait for the operating system. Until then, you can't use that system. But, if you are in a haste, by not allowing the system to finish booting properly, you execute your task on the computer, and you will end up giving the system a short life. Secondly, that system is prone to hang, always. Without the operating systems, the PC is useless. Without God, how can you talk about a set time? Look around and you will see reason in what I say.

For instance, bananas have their own season of production. If the season is, say, June – August, and while you were young, you've never seen bananas in the market and in the market since you were young you never saw bananas in the months of November to March. All of a sudden, you go to a place where you see bananas from November to March. There is no need to be surprised, because God makes everything possible. If the banana was cultivated using irrigation and fertilizer and even carbide to fasten the ripening, will you say that it is not banana? No. There is no addition or subtraction to what you know to be a banana. It is the same thing, but the difference is what it contains as nutrients. There are chances that such bananas will give you cancer and other diseases. This one didn't wait for the appropriate season and is liable to cause diseases. Allow things to happen in its season. You will enjoy it and will not experience problems while using it. Don't force results out of nature. Try and fix yourself in the program of God. Make use of His software for He will prepare you for the right time and that right time is the set time. Wait for the right time for it doesn't take time for it to come. Don't forget what we discussed in the previous paragraphs. Every adversity has an expiry date. God doesn't take permission before He blesses you. Anytime He comes is the right time as it is the set time. God never came late in any activity. In any situation, He comes at the right time. Just because He didn't show up at that moment in flesh and blood doesn't mean that he didn't show up. It is just that it's not the set time for Him to come. God works with time and the time He comes is the set time. Stop being in this level of shabby thought! Go higher by operating in a higher frequency and you will understand better. He didn't appear because it wasn't the set time. Did He appear later? Yes. He did. Some would say that He came late. Can God be late? No! He does things in His own way to take His glory. Imagine a fire that was supposed to consume them all became air conditioner to their bodies. He made history. Wait for the set time because God is never late.

12. BIG MAMA SUCCESS

Hello big mama "SUCCESS!"

Good morning madam! I am always loyal. I have been hearing a lot about you and how you do things. What makes me become interested in you is the way your name sounds out here, just like Mr. President! How were you able to create this awesome fame? I am still wondering. As old as you are, you are ever fresh and new! When I go to primary schools, pupils say that they want to be like mama success! When I go to the market, the apprentice learning a trade says that he wants to be like mama success! I asked what was so special about Mama Success. Anybody you breed is a winner, a champion, a hero, a legend – and above all else, a great man.

Please, Mama Success, I want to ask you a question. Who are you? To this, Mama Success said, "I am a woman with many children. My husband is Mr. RISK and my two sons are GOAL and DREAM. I have finished training them in school and today, they are renowned men in society. If you don't come close to them, you will definitely miss your track to me. If you want to reach me, come close to my husband and my sons. Capture me like the philistines captured Samson. If you want to know me better, meet my husband. Ask my husband RISK any question that you want to direct to me."

Success means different things to different people, but one thing in common is that everyone who has attained it has had a vision and the zeal to realize it. They have electrifying ideas, immense creativity and unlimited energy.

"I am the woman that carves out my own world. I am a woman that turns all obstacles into stepping stones."

S = Selecting your Goals

U = Unlocking your unlimited potential

C = Come out of your comfort zone

C = Confronting challenges confronting you

E = Expecting challenges

S = Saying no to shame, fear and distraction

S = Surrendering to God for He has the final say.

Sow your seeds because they have the ability to germinate and become a forest.

Don't listen to people because you are the one to answer yourself when you succeed or fail. People don't take you serious until you make them understand that you are serious. When you start something, seize the seriousness to conquer at the end. People will follow you. SUCCESS is in your hand. Unveil your unlimited potential and seize every opportunity that comes your way in life, because Mr. Opportunity is the only chance you have to succeed. Don't join the crowd that says success is by luck. It is not by chance. Think big and work tirelessly. Certainly, there will be positive results. SUCCESS is not based on revenue alone. It's beyond that. There is more wisdom in failure.

13. DREAM

1. A dream is a series of thoughts, images, and sensations occurring in a person's mind during sleep. "I had a recurrent dream about falling from great heights"

   Synonyms: fantasy, nightmare; vision, hallucination, daydream, reverie, trance, daze, stupor, haze, hypnotic state, half-conscious state, state of unreality;

2. A cherished aspiration, ambition, or ideal. "I fulfilled a childhood dream when I became champion"

   Synonyms: ambition, aspiration, hope; Goal, design, plan, aim, object, objective, grail, holy grail, target, intention, intent; Desire, wish, notion, yearning; Daydream, fantasy;

3. Dreams can be extraordinarily vivid or very vague; filled with joyful emotions or frightening imagery; focused and understandable or unclear and confusing.

Dream is also the propeller that propels you to success. Don't underestimate your dream. God is a big dreamer. He loves those that dream big, too. It like this. Someone imagined a car like Carl Benz. Henry Ford did too, and drew it. It was put into an architectural plan before it was manufactured. Today, men in the world enjoy it. Someone dreamt of it and made it a reality. It's more or less bringing those your imaginations to reality. You must put efforts to make your dream a reality. It may take time, but focus and concentration makes it a reality. Don't be afraid of mockery, because every dream sounds idiotic at first, to the ears of the second person.

Don't stop people from laughing at your dream! They will be the ones to clap for you, patronize you and benefit from it at the end. Did you see what happened to Joseph the dreamer when he told his brothers that they would bow before him and they laughed, asking themselves how that was possible. Joseph was the second last out of twelve. It would be the firstborn which is Ruben they would bow first. Where was Joseph in this? See how idiotic their thought could be! They concluded that it was idiotic for Joseph to come up. They saw it as an insult to their person and sold him.

Don't afraid when men call your dream idiotic. Carry on. When you attain success, they will be the ones to clap for you. Don't be afraid or feel bad about challenges. Your challenge might be a way of catapulting you to your dream land. Remember, dream land is far and you need something to catapult you there.

Look at Joseph. What if the parents don't have money to sponsor his trip? It was written that he would be a king in a foreign land. How could he have known the country if he was avoiding or running away from challenges? His challenges became his passport. In fact, his challenges catapulted him to the right land. He became something that would make those brothers bow down before him for the dream to come through.

DREAM MEANS

D = DESPERATION: A desperate man is an angry man capable of doing anything. Being desperate is not bad, but when it's used for negativity, it becomes bad.

R = READY: To be ready is to be in belligerent vitality. If you are desperate and not ready, it has no meaning. You must be ready to fulfill all righteousness, whether difficult or not. The readiness gives you moral to enter.

E = ENTER: Are you ready to enter? When you enter, you will be able to know how to strike. A desperate man who is not ready to enter is an empty threat. If you refuse to enter your being ready is just in vain.

A = ACTION: Action means effort. Actions speak louder than words. Action is the only major keyword and other words are peripheries.

M = MEASURE: Sit down to count your blessings. Take stock of your success so far.

The nitty-gritties of success involves integrating and understanding the paralysis of the whole story. When you are desperate, you have to be ready to enter into action. Then, measure it. That is why the holy book records that you should count your blessings and name them one by one and it will surprise you what you have achieved already. Nobody will lead you to the part of chaos in life with this understanding. Facts could be the truth, but the truth is always truth and can't be a fact. To be worthy of success, count how many people who came to her home through you.

The distance between you and your dream is just now and THEN, divided by TIME multiplied by EFFORT. The formula is:

(NOW and THEN) X EFFORT

TIME

In the game of success, effort and time matters too, so be careful. There is nothing like LUCK in the journey to success.

ATTITUDE, KNOWLEDGE, LEADERSHIP and EFFORT are the most important tools.

A	B	C	D	E	F	G	H	I	J
1	2	3	4	5	6	7	8	9	10

K	L	M	N	O	P	Q	R	S	T
11	12	13	14	15	16	17	18	19	20

U	V	W	X	Y	Z
21	22	23	24	25	26

Let's do a small exercise. Take the words: LUCK, ATTITUDE, KNOWLEDGE, LEADERSHIP and EFFORT. Be tenacious and determined. Do not give up easily. Talent, hard work and tenacity are crucial to career success.

L. U. C. K.

12% + 21% + 3% + 11% = 47%

A T T I T U D E

1% + 20% + 2% + 9% + 20% + 21% + 4% + 5% = 100%

K N O W L E D G E

11% +14% +15% +23%+12% +5% +4% +7% + 5% = 96%

L E A D E R S H I P

12% +5% +1% +4% +5% +18%+19%+8% +9% +16% = 84%

E F F O R T

5% + 6% + 6% + 15% + 18% + 20% = 70%

This means that ATTITUDE, KNOWLEDGE, LEADERSHIP and EFFORT know the road SUCCESS.

1. **KNOWLEDGE:** According to the Oxford English Dictionary, knowledge is information and skill gained through experience or education. It could be considered the total of what is known. It could be the awareness gained by experience of fact or situation. It is an idea of ideas integrated at your Training arena. Learning is an ornament in prosperity, a refuge in adversity and a provision in old age, says Aristotle. Learning is dangerous, says Alexander Pope. A little knowledge can make a difference. Your training arena could be SCHOOL, MARKET, OFFICE, TRAVEL, CHURCH, CONFERENCES AND SEMINARS.

In what way do you pay to obtain knowledge in all these? In the arena of learning, you either pay with your money or time or both.

a. SCHOOL: Before you obtain anything from school, you must pay your fees. After paying money, you must attend school - (so you pay with your time also.
b. MARKET: To gain knowledge from the market, you pay with time. Time is money.
c. OFFICE: In the office, you pay with time.
d. TRAVEL: Travelling is part of learning. You must pay for your ticket and deposit your time by making the journey.
e. JAIL: Here, you have different rules, reasoning, behaviours, mindset and other things. When come out, either you become worse or better. You pay with time and cash.

f. CHURCH: A place of worship, where we assemble to praise God, a school where we learn and train spiritually. One-tenth called (TITHE) holy book records in Malachi 3:10, is to be paid. When you pay your tithe, and give your offerings to the church, it means that you've paid money to get knowledge. Some ask about those who don't pay the tithe. In one way or the other, the fellow must give offering by free will.

g. CONFERENCES and SEMINARS: They are also places of learning. Before attending any seminar or conference you must pay for it. By paying to attend the conference or seminar, you pay for the knowledge. Knowledge is power only when utilized.

2. **LEADERSHIP:** It is the act of having control over a group of people. It is also having control or a final say over the group. In the journey of success, leadership is needed because you need to be in control to give adequate guidance that will propel you to success. When you lead well, it calls for promotion and recognition. You must expect difficulties and challenges because in most matters, there will be your role to decide. As a leader, when you do something and people do not like it, and are discussing or criticizing you, stop because it isn't worth it. When you are being discussed, it means you are well announced. When you are well announced, people love to know who you are. The Holy book records in (Mathews 5:14–16): "Let your light so shine before men, that they may see your good works and glorify your father which is in heaven." Just a look at these tips it unveils an important principle. The holy book didn't say let your light so shine before men. All men, not some men, that they may see your good work and glorify your father in heaven. Your mandate is: "You should let your light shine anywhere and everywhere you found yourself." Joseph the son of Jacob was put in prison after being wrongly accused. Yet, he shone brightly in the midst of all his difficult times. Eventually, he rose to become the Prime Minister of a foreign land. The inevitable result is that through you, the lives of others will be affected and improved. The scripture doesn't say that men will see your good work and promote or reward you. The holy book says that that they will glorify your father who is in heaven,

who in turn will promote you. Your promotion comes from the lord. Psalm 75: 6. Do what's right. It won't be long before you're catapulted to higher dimensions of greatness and prosperity. To be a great leader, you must be a servant because leaders are servants.

3. **EFFORT:** It means when an unusual amount of physical or mental energy is needed to do it.
4. **ATTITUDE:** Your attitude towards something is the way you think and feel about it, especially when this is shown in the way you behave. If you refer to someone as a friend with attitude, they have a striking and individual style of behavior. If something is at a particular altitude it is a height above sea level. Your attitude determines your attitude, said Jeff Keller, the founder and President of Attitude is Everything. He defines attitude as the mental filter through which you experience the world. He also says, furthermore, that some people see the world through the filter of Optimism (the glass being half-full) while others see life through a filter of pessimism (the glass being half-empty) Hugh Downs says that "Happy is not a person in a certain set of circumstances but rather a person with a certain set of attitude."

It is only you who has the power to control your attitude. Nobody else. Charles Pipestone says: "You cannot always control circumstances but you can control your own thoughts. Maintain a positive attitude until you get the right result."

14. LIFE PURPOSE/JOURNEY OF LIFE

Life is a journey and every moment in life is food for thought. Shakespeare said, “Always, the dullness of a fool is the whetstone of the wits. A child is not a vase to be filled but a fire to be lit.”

Ernest Dimnet: “of consciousness varying with readers”.

“You start to live when you commit your life to cause higher than yourself. You must learn to depend on divine power for the fulfillment of a higher calling.”

—Lailah Gifty Akita

“Sometimes the best journeys are those, that start when we do not plan, continue how we do not expect and are taking us places we do not know.”

—Aisha Mirza

“When you travel, take many photographs of the place to have a historical memories of the place.”

—Lailah Gifty Akita

Maybe the best things are those that take the most work, you know? Maybe how you get somewhere can be at least as important as where you’re going.”

—Ryan North

“We must dare to rise above the obstacles on our path.”

—Lailah Gifty Akita

“Destiny’s Gate is filled with darkness and light. If you identify with the darkness, this is a good sign as we all have to embrace the darkness within us in order to heal and be brought into the Light as One.”

—Lee Bice-Matheson,

"When you follow the right steps you will never get lost."

—Lailah Gifty Akita

Life is a journey filled with lessons, hardships, heartaches, joys, celebrations and special moments that will ultimately lead us to our destination, our purpose in life. The road will not always be smooth; in fact, throughout our travels, we will encounter many challenges.

For you to journey through life so many things are involved.

Swami Vivekananda said: "Happiness presents itself before man, wearing the crown of sorrow on its head. He who welcomes it must also welcome sorrow." Life is a journey where you see both, good and bad, rough and smooth. In the journey of life, don't say that you are more than fortunate because the breeze of goodies blew your way too early. There are people who were fortunate to get the goodies of life early on, while some get theirs much later. All of them are goodies. The difference there is in time – but when you think about it, there is nothing like late or early, anytime it comes is the right time. In the journey of life, what you should calculate is: How well greater than how far is equal to success.

(How well < How far) = success.

We don't calculate: how far but we calculate how well.

A man worked for 30 years of his life for the government and retired. The government gave him $5 million as his gratuity. Another man, his classmate finished school and was jobless for 15 years. All of a sudden, a friend met him at a mall. After their interaction, he gave him a contract of $500 million. When he finished, he earned $200 million. The other fellow travelled. No one could notice him until after 17 years. He came back and built estates and companies worth hundreds of million dollars.

For a third person, his father gave him $20 million to start a business. He finished school and after 15 years, he couldn't account for the money spent. In all these calculations, you will find that it wasn't how far or how well. Even if it takes times for the goodies of life to locate you, don't worry. It doesn't matter. The journey of life is long. Don't get worried and just stick to what you believe in. Put in effort and the right attitudes. You will get there. Some men withdraw from the journey. Some stop on the way. Some see the bad side and the roughness of the road and decided to commit suicide. Some can't bear the pain and decide to pack up. Remember, at the end of every tunnel, there is light. Only you can summon patience, courage and be steadfast. With that, you will definitely see light. Find a reason to get to the end of the tunnel.

The journey of life begins as soon a child is born. To confirm if the child is alive, the child must cry. When he cries his first cry, the mother and father are happy. In life, you must expect problems. They are challenges that make you strong. It is the fuel that keeps you going till you reach the end of the tunnel. When you are on the journey of life, men will laugh at you and mock you, but you should not stop moving because they were mocking you. I am saying this is because if you are already on your way to quit, just because of what you are hearing from the men around you, be strong. Don't look back.

Life is only one. Nobody has two lives. You can't accomplish your dream without a goal. Remember, to dream is to be desperate to enter into action. You will enjoy the action when you measure it. It is what propels you to success. Set your goals because they are your target! Before you get your target, you must visualize it. You must have a vision. It is easy to have a vision, but if you have vision you must be focused. How can you have focus when you don't have reason to focus? You must first have reason to propel you towards reality. If you were asked why you do what you do, you would say what is best known to you. If you were asked, "Why are you living?" What would your answer be? To live is to exist. Find one or two reasons: Are you living to affect lives or destroy lives? If you look at it critically, you observe that good and bad help each other! How? Listen to this small story.

A man in uniform apprehended a group of armed robbers during an operation. When they were punished by the uniformed men, (the Police officer asked the robbers: "Why do you do what you did? The robbers said, "Sir, we are creating employment!" "How?" the Police Officer asked. The robbers replied saying, "Sir, if not for our activities will the government give you work? If not us, how many years would you spend looking for work? You would probably be jobless. If not, would you have known anything or touch the gun in the name of pursuing us? Now you enjoy a whole Prado Jeep XUV just because of us. You have a car but you are enjoying a costly jeep. Last year alone, how many policemen were recruited to be in service to look for people like us?" "120 men!" said the officer. The robbers burst into laughter and said, "It is like a movie! You were busy bullying the men who put you in the post of a Police Officer. What would your situation have been if you were still jobless?" The policemen were shocked and told their men to take the robbers before court.

When they got to court, the judge asked, "Young men, why do you do what you did?" They said, "Creating jobs!" "Really?" the judge asked. "How do you mean?" The robbers said, "My lord, just last year, 120 men were employed in the force by the government for our sake. If not us, I wonder what those jobless fellows would have done today! My Lord, are we not doing our part in society since the government is not doing anything about employment?" The Judge was flabbergasted and was speechless. The judge ordered that they be put in jail. The investigation went on.

All newcomers in jails are bombarded with many questions. As soon as they were put into jail, the superintendent asked, "Young men, what were you accused of?" The robbers said, "Sir, creating jobs!" "Creating jobs and you were put in jail? I am going to sue the judge, for this partial judgment!" The chief jailer got went to the judge and said, "My Lord, I am disappointed in you. How could you have prosecuted those boys for giving people jobs. Jobs are tough to procure!" The judge said, "Those boys? Don't mind them! They were apprehended by the police on the road, robbing people!" The superintendent was shocked. He went back to jail and ordered the boys to be beaten up heavily.

After five days, one of them became ill. He was taken to hospital. The doctor asked, "Why were you beaten up?" The robber said, "We are creating jobs everywhere we go!" The doctor asked, "What rubbish! I heard what happened!" The robbers said, "For the sake of our being on the highway, 120 men got jobs as police officers last year by the government. For the sake of our appearance in court, some young men read law and can practice law in court. The government knew about us and built a jail to give more jobs for other people. Now, more than 120 jailors were recruited to make sure that we don't escape. When I asked a jailor why he was following us, they told us that they were doing their duty, of course." The doctor asked, "How does all this affect my profession?" The robber said, "Now I am not well. I am so sick that I give you a job to do, by asking you to cure me! Without me, how would you do your job? How would you get paid?"

The doctor wondered, "How can a robber give me a job!" The doctor never understood the angle that the robbers were going on about. He gave the robber an injection. The man who sold caskets said, "God I need some customers." Who does he want to die so that he could sell his casket? God answered his prayers. The doctor killed one of the robbers. When they went to buy the casket, the seller thanked God and the robbers for purchasing his product. With that money, he could pay his daughter's school fees. To get his next income, he would be waiting for another person to die.

The judge heard what happened. He issued their summons and said, "What is the need for forgiveness when there is no sin? What is the need for money if you can't spend it? What is the need for keeping food when we are not expecting hunger? Why do we build hospitals if we don't want people to get sick? Why do we sell coffins when we don't want people to die? Why do we have the police when we don't expect a crime? Why do we have lawyers when we don't want to have the accused? There is no paralysis in all of these analyses.

Some people would say that life is the air we breathe in. Without the air we breathe in, there is no life. If some say this is what they understand life to be, what do you understand life to be? To some people, life is taken to be a "market", because to them, life is like a big market where you come, buy and go or come to sell and go. These men always think of business and transactions. They don't think of anything else. It is their belief and they live for it. Another set understand and take life to be a "Party". To them life is a club or disco where you dance and enjoy yourself. In their mind, fun means to have sex, drink, smoke and what not. These men understand as being enjoyment and nothing else.

There are those who understand and take life to be tourism, because life is like an adventure. To them, life is a place to give our eyes a good treat by sightseeing. These men will say that life is a teacher. They see life as a university where you learn and gather experience. Some men take life to be a marathon race. These are men that believe that anywhere a man with four-wheels reaches, a man with ten toes is capable of reaching. It only takes time. These men believe that life is a journey. They believe one needs to drive slowly and steadily, as otherwise there will be a crash. Some understand and take life like a soldier - come soldier go woman, born again! They believe that life is all about reproduction. It is all about giving birth to new ones and multiplying the world like the holy book instructed in the book of Mark.

Life to some people, is a game. If you know "Cheers in Door" well, you will understand that it has rules. They believe that if you play your role in life, you win, and that playing by the rules means that the trophy is yours. The deal is that nobody can beat them with their style, no matter what. Some say that life is a teacher. To them, life is full of learning. These men say, once you stop learning you start dying. Some say that life is just like computer garbage, meaning what you give in you must take. To these set of men, what you put in as an input is what you get as an output. What do you take life as? Choose from any of theirs, or frame your own. Good and bad work together to produce results. Always choose the good one because it pays. Don't follow the crowd. Don't admire the bad, admire the good. It pays to do well. Don't give reasons for why you commit a crime. There is always a way in a daunting situations. Choose to obey the law, because nobody is above the law! Don't follow the crowd. Start using your brains. Stop following start exploding!

15. COMPLIMENTS

COMPLIMENT

A polite expression of praise or admiration.

"She paid me an enormous compliment"

Synonyms: flattering remark, tribute, accolade, commendation, bouquet, pat on the back, encomium; Praise, acclaim, acclamation, plaudits, admiration, approbation, homage, eulogy; Congratulations or praise expressed to someone. "My compliments on your cooking"; Flattery, blandishments, blarney, honeyed words; trade last; rare laudation, eulogium;

"She blushed at the unexpected compliment"

Antonyms: insult, criticism, an act or circumstance that implies praise or respect.

"It's a compliment to the bride to dress up on her special day"

Synonyms: congratulations, praise, commendations; Informal kudos; "My compliments on your cooking"

Formal greetings, especially when sent as a message.

"Carry my compliments to your kinsmen"

Synonyms: greetings, good wishes, best wishes, regards, respects, salutations, felicitations; archaic remembrances; archaic devoirs; "Lady Margaret sent her compliments to him"

Verb: compliment; 3rd person present: compliments; past tense: complimented; past participle: complimented; gerund or present participle: complimenting; Politely congratulate or praise (someone) for something. "He complimented Erika on her appearance".

Praise (something politely) "The manager was heard complimenting the other team's play."

Synonyms: praise, sing the praises of, heap praise on, pay tribute to, speak highly/well of, flatter, say nice things about, express admiration for, wax lyrical about, make much of, congratulate, commend, acclaim, pat on the back, take one's hat off to, throw bouquets at, applaud, salute, honour, eulogize, extol:

Black English: Big someone/something up; dated cry someone/something up, crack someone/something up; archaic emblazon; rare laud, panegyrize, felicitate "Critics fell over themselves to compliment his performance"

Antonyms: criticize, condemn

Present someone with (something as a mark of courtesy. "Prince George expected to be complimented with a seat in the royal coach"

Compliment: According to the Oxford English dictionary it means: an expression of praise or admiration. Formal greetings.

When you do what you do, what are the motives behind your actions? Why do you do the things you do? How do you do them? The motivation behind your aspiration matters. There are certain things you must do in other to win one's heart. They are:

1. Love
2. Compliment

Let's start with LOVE. What is LOVE? According to the Oxford English dictionary love is a strong feeling of affection or a great interest and pleasure in something. Are you in love? Are you ready to fall in love? How jealous are you? How romantic are you? Love yourself. It is simply the law of attraction. Some will ask: How do I know if the one I love has the same feelings for me? Whenever she does something like this you don't need to be told again.

a. If she becomes sad because of your sadness or anger.
b. If she doesn't get angry when you contradict her opinion.
c. If she always consults you before she makes a decision.
d. If she always tries to make conversation with you.
e. If she always tries to help you or does some of your tasks.

f. If she gets happy when you gift her something even if it's very simple.
g. If she worries about you in your absence.
h. If she cares to do what pleases you, and never repeats what angers you.
i. If she doesn't care about how little you earn (money)
j. If she patiently bears the harm you cause
k. If she likes to share what you like and cares to become a part of your world.
l. If she doesn't feel shy around you.
m. If she always gives you good news personally instead of you hearing from a third party.

Love is the richest of all treasures. Without it, there is nothing. With it, there is everything Love never perishes, even if the bones of a lover are ground fine like powder. Just as the perfume of sandalwood does not leave it, even if it is completely ground up, the basis of love is the soul. It is indestructible, and therefore eternal. Beauty can be destroyed but not love.

In a compliment for instance, if you see a lady you admire and would love to woo, what do you do first? Do you just start by just bossing over her? She won't respond to your nonsense. But when you see her, first smile at her if she responses, you can then start complimenting her by admiring her. You can admire her teeth, her shoes, her dress, her eyes, her hair and even her perfume. Tell her that she is the most beautiful thing that could even happen to you only if she could give her two minutes. Talk to her just express your feelings. Tell her that she was the most beautiful thing that ever happened to the world. If she would allow you to say all this, you have actually seen someone you can die for! Even if this girl or lady is a witch, believe me she must listen to you. Now ask her, please Chioma or Ukay, which part of heavens did you come from because you are imagining if she escape from heaven just to drive you crazy. Ask her was it God that sent her or she decided to come on her own? Tell her that what you admire most in her is the way she seats charily and cheerfully when you know very well that she was making lots of noise ha ha ha ha ha. Now tell me a lady you praise like this wouldn't ask you who you are? Definitely she would even if she is a devil. You see through compliment to her you were able to draw her attention to tell her you're in my mind. Everywhere this lady sees you, she would be admiring you too even if she hates you before. This is to tell you that everybody likes compliment. Let's assume you have some men you are controlling. If you come and you don't give them compliment don't expect more from them. You can get all their powers and strength to work through your compliment. If you send them on a mission and they came back without full expectations from them, don't just start correcting them without first complimenting them because by so doing, you will win their heart and whatever correction that is given to them would be implemented. But if you are a leader and you don't give compliments believe me you wouldn't lead well. It is like when you are correcting a teen without love and compliment, definitely he wouldn't listen to you.

Look at a young boy who happened to be interviewed on a television channel about his president. He was busy giving compliments to his president when he knew that he was lacking funds. (This won the president's heart and he sent for the boy and gave him a federal job. When you compliment someone, don't support evil things. Say the truth as it will set you free. Everybody likes compliments. How do you feel when you dress up and come out and nobody admires or compliments you? Will you feel good when you get back home? You would think that you wore such expensive things on your body and nobody admired you. This is the same way a girl would dress up elegantly and gorgeously to come out and nobody says to her, "Sweetheart you are good!" Call out to her and say to her that she looks good. Learn to put a smile on someone's face by complimenting him or her. I know you wouldn't be happy if someone sees you dress up with costly shoes and says that you look ugly in those shoes. Even if you bought it for $1000, if you manage to go home with it, when that bad compliment echoes in your ears, you won't wear it again. Give compliments because everybody needs it.

If a man gives you something and you compliment him, I wonder how he wouldn't do more. That is why we are instructed to lavish praise on God with psalms and hymns and spiritual songs. For example, you say the lord is the strength of my life, so who shall I be afraid of? He strengthened me and made me a success. I walk in the light of God; therefore I'm the light of God! The next thing to do is sing and make a melody in your heart to the Lord. Give thanks always for all that He's done. Say beautiful things about (God and testify to His wondrous work in your life. Say, In the Name of Jesus Father, I bless your name; I thank you for your kindness, love grace and mercy! I thank you for promoting me in life and granting me spiritual blessings in heavenly places in Christ." Instead of complaining to God about your finances, family or job, learn to give compliments to Him because when your life is full of compliments you will have a triumphant life. God loves compliment and He is love.

Imagine when you compliment God and say "I blessed you Lord you are holy and forever you are God. I bless you heavenly father, I exalt your majesty; I worship you for your omniscience and your excellent splendor. I adore you for who you are not for what you are to me. To you be all glory and dominion forever!" If someone was there when you were complimenting God this way, if he has not given his life to Christ or doesn't know who God is at all, he would be forced in his heart to know who God is because of the way you were complimenting (God. For you to lavish such compliments to this deity, He must something unique to him! It might lead to him asking what the possibilities are for him to know your God?

Compliments build our spirit. It boosts our morale. It gives agility. It makes us feel important and removes fear. It makes us talk with boldness. It makes people see us with a different mindset. Compliments bring happiness. If someone compliments you, he puts a smile on your face. Does a sad fellow smile, let alone laugh? Here are six steps to happiness.

Think less and feel more

Talk less and listen more

Watch less and do more

Judge less and accept more

Complain less and appreciate more

Frown less and smile more.

Before you compliment anybody, look for the good in that person. The good you see is the basis of your compliment. One can complement your bad side too. Everybody is not all good and also everybody is not all bad. Try to see the good in others. What makes something bad? If someone is bad and good character is 50/50, there is a problem. It means that the person is half-devil and half-angel. If someone's bad character is greater than his good character, the logical conclusion applies to be bad. Otherwise, you will say that the person is good. It means that your good side is greater than your bad side. We can say he is good no matter how you see it. This kind of compliment comes whenever there is consideration in your good side. Nobody is a devil. The devil uses somebody. When he does, we say: "This man is a devil!" We mean that he is bad because he had already exhibited the devilish side which is bad. God is good, that is why He wants you to look out for the good in others. Philippians 4:8 Bible says: "Fix your thoughts on what is true and good and right. Think about things that are pure and lovely and dwell on the fine good things on others. Think about all you can praise God for and be glad about."

There are people who almost never see the good in others. They are known to dwell on the shortcomings in others. When others make good remarks about someone, they will inject something negative. For example, if someone is complimented for a girl for her dressing, a negative person would possibly say. "Yes her dress is beautiful, but she's overweight!" They would rather dwell on what they perceive as deficient rather than pay simple compliments even when deserved. What a wrong way of life or wrong way to live!

For the most part, such behaviours are signs of frustration. Those who act in this manner don't realize that the negative attitudes they exhibit can only entrench them deeper in misery. Frustrated people can't see the good in others, because they can't see the good in themselves. So, they often criticize and pick on others. Frustrated people don't know how to compliment others. What I told you in Philippians 4:8 is so important because observing and appreciating the good in others isn't about making them happy. Rather, it is about building a strong and positive character as you allow the outflow of good things from within you. It's about becoming joyful, successful and prosperous. Make a conscious effort to appreciate others for who they are. It's the right thing to do. Even when you notice something wrong in others, love enough to point it out sincerely. This is a virtue you must cultivate. It will place you on a higher plane in life. Just try it see good in someone today and compliment them.

16. THEM SAY

This must sound funny to you. But, never in your life, welcome "them say" in your house because them say has enough ability to destroy what you took time to build. "Them say" has the ability to render your God-created mind into a restless land. Them say can set your mind on what is not true and can never be true. Although it is said that in every rumour there is an atom of truth, the truth in them say could be exaggerated beyond your imagination and is baseless. Why is it so? Because, it moves from one mixture to another and another and another and doesn't stop. Mrs. Them Say is an old woman. She got married to Information Minister Hon'ble Chief Gossip and God blessed their union with four children. Their names are: Propaganda, Slander, Rumour, Blackmail

According to the Oxford English Dictionary:

PROPAGANDA: Information that is often biased or misleading used to promote a political cause or point of view.

SLANDER: The crime of saying something untrue that damages a person's reputation make false and damaging statements about someone.

RUMOUR: A story spread among a number of people which is unconfirmed and may be false.

BLACKMAIL: The demanding of money from someone in return for not revealing information that could disgrace them, the use of threats or other pressure to influence someone.

Mrs. Them say doesn't have legs, yet she walks more than anybody that has legs. She doesn't have a car yet she can drive. She doesn't have a jet yet she can travel from one country to another. She was the first that gave the Information Minister. Someone without legs has the ability to deliver to the neighbourhood a full blown catastrophe! She doesn't have a mouth yet can talk more than those that have mouths. She doesn't have tongue yet she has the ability and capabilities of destroying a whole nation! She is the only woman who can travel to any part of the world without a passport and visa. Who are you to stop her when she is on the move? She doesn't have siblings talk more of friends.

She is the only woman that can put two brothers in enmity. In science, the scientist says that madam Them Say could be said to be a chemical reaction where a new substance is found. It is not easily reversible. She always leaves an indelible mark. She can travel from one place to another and her behaviours change. If you have an issue with someone, when the third party comes in, she carries it to the fourth and the fourth to the fifth and so on. The third person was not there during the incident but would narrate the story as if he was there. The story is changing because of the pepper and salt added to attract the audience. It goes from gossip to rumour to slander to blackmail, all in the name of them say.

She moves like fire and consumes whatever blocks her way. She doesn't ask for forgiveness. Even if she asks for forgiveness, the deed is done and is irreversible. Wisdom makes a wise person more powerful than ten rulers in a city. There is no one on earth who is righteous, no one who does what is right or never sins. Jesus died and made anyone who believed him, perfect. Them say doesn't pay anybody. Be wise. Whatever exists is far off and most profound. Who can discover it? Turn your mind to investigate and to search for wisdom.

17. WHAT MONEY CAN DO!

MONEY: Who are you?

I AM A SPIRIT, I HAVE WINGS AND I CAN FLY. MEN SEE ME AS PAPER THAT THEY PUT IN THE BANK BUT NO I AM A SPIRIT I EXPRESS MYSELF IN A PAPER NOTES WHICH THE WORLD CALLED CURRENCIES IN ALL COUNTRIES OF THE WORLD.

For instants: you dollars used by USA,

CANADA ETC.

RINGGETS used by MALAYSIA.

PESO used by PHILIPINES, MEXICO, AGENTINA ETC.

RUPEES used by INDIA ETC.

NAIRA used by NIGERIA. EURO used by many EUROPIAN COUNTRIES.

POUNDS used by GREAT BRITAIN...

DINARS used by ALGERIA, KUWAIT ETC

DIRHAM used by UNITED ARAB EMIRATE.

LIRA used by TURKEY.

Take look at all these few countries mentioned above you will see that in all the different currencies that they are using still represent me (CHIEF MONEY) but in a paper note

Swami Vivekananda says: “Happiness presents itself before man, wearing the crown of sorrow on its head. He who welcomes happiness must also welcome sorrow.”

No pain no gain. IMAGINE WHAT MONEY IS SAYING... LAUGH AND LEARN FROM THIS JOKE:

Once upon a time an old man called Odawa was looking for Mr. Money. He lived in a distant country and decided to make a move on a pursuit of purpose to the country, looking for Mr. MONEY. As he traveled, Odawa saw the activities going on around him. It was too horrible and he was not able to join in. He saw men and women, ladies and gentlemen, boys, and girls even kings in the same activity in search of Mr. Money. Odawa stayed for a very long time waiting for Mr. Money to come, yet he didn't come. Odawa decided to have shift position where they told him that he would see. Mr. Money and the old man continued to the place. When he got there, he saw some men on the way that eventually stopped him with AK47s, because they thought he was with Mr. Money in his car. When the gentlemen opened the door, they saw only the old man. The gentlemen asked, "Where is Mr. Money? We have been on this road since the morning, waiting for him." The old man said, "I am also searching for him that is why I am on this journey." (The gentlemen let him to go and instructed that if he succeeded in seeing (Mr. Money, he should let them know. "But sir," asked the gentleman. "Where is his home town? Could you show me?" They started saying some nonsense, not knowing that Mr. Money was hearing them and laughed. Mr. Odawa told the gentlemen not to worry that once he got to his home town and saw Mr. Money, he would come back and inform them. The men thanked the old man profoundly. After the promise Odawa made to those boys, while on his way to Mr. Money's hometown, it was dark and he had no option but to sleep. Just then, Mr. Money appeared and said, "My friend, don't waste your time and energy thinking that the place you are about going isn't my home town. Settle anywhere you can and I will visit you. You can go back and tell the gentlemen that I don't have a native place. I visit whom I want to visit and I stay anywhere you can think off in the world." The old man got angry and asked (Mr. Money who he was. Mr. Money laughed and said: "I am a spirit. I have every power and immunity to make you or mare you. I have wings and can fly. I make things happen! In this life, after God, count on me. Tell me what you can do without me (When people say life is good and enjoyable because I am there, when men desire good houses, how can they build it without me?" (When a Young boy woke up and said he needed a beautiful, elegant and charming lady now tell me how he could have got her without my signature (Mr. Money).

Even if the young boy succeeds in getting the lady without me (Mr. Money) wow wonder what will happen because wisdom men said if love comes from the door and didn't meet me (Mr. money) the love will jump from the window. That is why I told men that I am the only reason why your so called wife would live you for another man. If she didn't succeed would be opening her laps for other men just because her husband didn't give her enough me (Mr. Money) and buy posh cars and build a good house.

I am the only reason why a young girl would have sex with 10 to 20 men in a day in the name of prostitution just to get me. I (Mr. Money) is the only reason men betray a fellow friend. If you don't have me (Mr. Money) believe me no friend for you. Why did I say so? Yes because no one would love to come where he would see nothing or rather suffer. Ha haahahhah but when you have me the sky is not your limit but your starting point. See my dear with me (Mr. Money) the whole world is in your palm because if you don't have me you must look empty and worthless in the site of men. Someone will tell you that I Mr. money is everything but the question is: tell me exactly what you can do without me chief money? For that thing to be successful you know that I Mr. Money must be involved for it to worthwhile or is it because I don't want to tell you before that I am chief?

Little wonder men call everybody that you know that got me (Mr. Money) a CHIEF.

Hahahahahaah wow so nice.

I am a chief do you know? In case you don't know it's better you start knowing from today!

I Chief money the honorable chief is the only chief that can make a man to sell his conscience. For your earlier information in other for you to become whatever you want to become it is me who will make it happen. The honorable chief money huh wows. Even if you manipulate it without me (chief money) you still must need me for maintenance.

If you can tell yourself the truth, what possibly can you maintain in this life without me chief money? Mention it, is it so called beautiful house, posh car or your beautiful wife? Just try to avoid me (chief money) and see where your wife would be and see what she would possibly turn into or look like. Surely she will look like hail...

Hahahahhaha. Yes like I often say I am the only thing that can make you above your equals.

I can give respect that was denied from you for years just immediately they see me chief money both the oldest man even you so called king would bow to you. Do you know why? Just because I am also and a king salutes fellow king because I am the back born of his kingship without me he will have no voice.

They would give you all manner of titles in my name. Hahahahahahaha.

Chief money talks! I build homes and also destroys homes. Chief money is the only thing that can make a woman leave her matrimonial home for another man, for sex not because she wants to be satisfied but because she needed me, Chief money, from the hands of the so-called chief she went to meet. I summon issues. In our generation, if you speak good grammar and put your hand in your pocket from now till tomorrow, if you don't have Chief money, you are nobody. No matter how many degrees you have, with your beautiful grammar, no speech you make will have weight. If you like make 101 reasonable suggestions, those suggestions are errors of the highest order in the sight of others because you don't have me (money! Let an illiterate or a full grown idiot who happens to have (money say anything - it's always good and welcoming. Men clap at his stupidity for credibility. They will tell you that a wise man is talking. They call him the son of the soil. Are you wise? If you are a wise man, capture Chief money. If you don't capture Chief money. You are not a wise man. If you were wise, why didn't you capture chief money?

Chief money says: "capture me and I will make you wise in the eyes of men in the world!

18. HOW WONDERFULLY GOD CAN BLESS A COUNTRY

God blessed Nigeria with all kinds of mineral resources. How useful are those endowments to her as a nation? She has crude oil, lead ore, Zinc, Tin, Copper, coal, clay, Stones, Aluminum and other things. The whole world knows that she is endowed with all these and more. If a father has possession of two big estates containing 100 seven-storey buildings in each, and telecommunication company, shipping company, oil and gas, four five star hotels, airline, hospital, university and a radio station is owned by him, even if the man has 20 wives and each has 10 (children, his children won't suffer or labour in life. But do you know that prematurity can make one of the children to start asking for his share before time? Prematurity has caused many deaths of many people and countries. Prematurity is a disease that has killed so many people and countries. The holy book records the prodigal son and his activities. When a child is growing and he is not at the age to handle issues and says to his father, "Give me my share of your wealth I want to take over. I think I am at the age of maturity and can handle things on my own!" What do you think? Maybe this boy is still at secondary school and the father wants to see him through to higher education.

Things that can Commonly Lead to Premature Freedom

1. LOVE: Love can make the father give him that freedom without knowing that it is premature.
2. HATRED: Hatred could make the father to do so.
3. When a child is loved by the father so much, it could lead to premature freedom.
4. When a child proves too stubborn could lead to premature freedom
5. When a child thinks he knows more than the father, it could lead to premature freedom.
6. When a child is proud and pompous, it could lead to premature freedom.

Mama Africa is not happy because of the stupidity of some of her children, so-called African countries. Nigeria is the giant of Africa. She has almost all the mineral resources God left before He rested. She has best brain in the world another Garden of Eden. But hunger kills the citizenry. Take a look at this illustration. Mr. A always goes to the pub and $1000, but every night his children eat poorly and to bed. Mr. B always goes to the pub and spends $1000, and his children beg on the street. Mr. C goes to the beer parlor, spends $1000 and the wife and the children are happy because dad spends money on them heavily and makes them comfortable. They don't care what and where dad spends money outside.

Prematurity is what made some African countries to get premature freedom. Like some countries in West Africa, many of her children are scattered all over the world like children without a mother.

When the prodigal son requested his share of his father's wealth, he was premature to handle things. He intended on getting his freedom not knowing that the kind of freedom he wanted to get was premature. His father's love gave him his premature freedom and he left with the wealth to an unknown land and squandered it all. When life posted him to the land of suffering, he remembered where his water pot started leaking. He realised that asking for his share was not a sin but he was too premature to handle it, so he failed. Despite possibilities of rejection, he summoned courage to go back and learn.

When a child that feels that she upto age to do whatever she likes and nobody should or can question her, check out off 100%, it was only 2–3% that I saw escaped from being idiots at the end of the day. Yes 2–3% you would say after all some people became somebody after, they settle down remember 3% is not a pass mark. If you eventually get 3% as a mark in an examination, it is as good as you didn't take the exam. I don't know if you will shamefully tell your friend that you got 3% as a mark in exam. If it was, it is as good as you didn't take the exam. I don't know if you will shamefully tell your friend that you got 3% mark. If afterwards she was given that opportunity to rock that so called life style and at the end of the day no wealth left to stand on after his mistake, what will he do? The question is for Nigeria as one of the daughters of mama Africa. Do you want to make the whole mistake in the world before you realized that you are now an adult not a child again? Remember that you are now an adult not a child again? Remember that you are more or less an old woman now not a girl nor lady again. I believe a woman of 54 years had entered menopause for what I know and giving birth at this age… I don't know. Unless by miracle like the one that was recorded in the holy book mama Sarah who gave birth at the age 90 years and you know that a woman of 90 years rarely eat meat in this generation.

I believe that a child of nursery school is expected to behave like a nursery pupil. This stage of a child I believed he might be urinating on the Pampers as well going to toilet therein. His activities are not based on alphabet or numbers rather learning to pronounce mummy, father, aunty, Uncle. Everything about that child would be based on how to call his daddy and mummy and if the parent hears that the child is calling mummy and daddy as a result of attending that school, they will retain that child knowing full well that by the time that child would enter into primary level, the child would be reading the 26 alphabets and atleast numbers 1–100,000/- if not 1,000,000,000 not only reading it as well write them. Now a child of primary school is expected not to urinate in his panties or wear pampers again.

Note: if the child does that, punish him once or twice he would put to stop on it knowing fully well that if he does that again he was going to be punished and he knows the pains of punishment.

Now Nigeria is 55 years still urinating on her panties! What do you have to say? A child in secondary school expected to read and write things, construct good grammar, write letters and so on and so forth but what Nigeria knows at the age 55 years is not to write letters but to write money bills and expenses not the income. Write how they spend 10 billion dollars on electricity as power sector yet there is no where you will enter in Nigeria homes that don't have this small generator. Yet she supply power to almost all the neighbouring countries. No power even in the Federal capital territory, you can imagine sometime power sieze. She will write only on the newspaper that she spent 20 billion dollars on construction of roads. Who told you? And you agreed that it was built? Ha ha ha never you listen to that my dear the road was built on the News Papers and that 20 billion dollars you heard was not lies. It was real but the road would be built on the News Papers and the money is shared among two to ten set of men of which we know who got the lion share of that public fund ha ha ha ha ha. The money was transferred to Switzerland account. Don't say that I said. You really want to know? What happened to one of her late president? During the regime of one of her presidents, some of the fund dumped in some countries by Mr. President was realized. Yes was on the newspaper. Okay just imagine the kind of money one dumped somewhere and we were told that just some were realized and that some federal government dogged their hand inside the fund and bought jeep worth 50 thousand dollar each to her police stations in the entire country and the fund was still remaining. My God. Did I tell you anything? The one that remain, what was it used for? Don't ask me go and ask her.

This is the only kind of letter she could write. What about the good grammar the child was expected to speak? Her grammar isn't based on English, but money. Her grammar is just being a good listener in the here and now.

The federal government spent like I told you before. It was in the newspapers. The whole world confirms that Nigeria must be heaven on earth, or the garden of Eden. You hear the governors saying: "I spent 15 billion dollars on road construction!" And yet, no road leads even to his house. At least if a road lead to his house was constructed, many living around him would benefit. But, there was none. Now he sees that the fleets of XUVs he bought for his convoy do not have good roads. He could have driven the cars he bought if he had good roads. So he chooses to buy a private jet for himself and his family. Even as at they choose to fly, they still die in the air. The man will speak his own grammar, saying that he pumped in $20 million in the health sector. But if he has a headache, he runs abroad. Does somebody who eats at the restaurant everyday cooks at home at all? If he does, what should warrant him eating out always?

Back to what I was telling you in my illustration. A child in secondary school is no longer writing the alphabet, or reading numbers. Now, he is expected to know how to add zeros to numbers:

e.g. 0, 1, 2, 3, 4, 5, 6, 7, 8, 9, 1 + 0 = 10, 1 + 00 = 100 and so on.

3; 13; 113; 11360

TTH	TH	H	T	U
				3
			1	3
		1	1	3
1	1	3	6	0

We know mathematically 3 = 3 units

13 = Ten + Three 10 + 3 = 13 One tenth and 3 unit

113 = One hundred + Ten + Three = 100 + 10 + 3 = 113 One hundred one tenth and 3 unit.

11360 = Eleven thousand + Three hundred + Sixty

Any number that you add zero to, is in trouble. I will just add one zero to it. See how many numbers it will jump! Let's try it now.

1 + 0 = 10

1 + 00 = 100

1 + 000 = 1,000

1 + 0000 = 10,000

1 + 00000 = 100,000

1 + 000000 = 1,000,000

1 + 0000000 = 10,000,000

1 + 00000000 = 100,000,000

1 + 000000000 = 1,000,000,000

Till infinity.

This was taught with other subjects. She never learnt any other subject save for English and Mathematics. That is why she put it as a compulsory subject. Even if you pass other subject and don't pass

English and Mathematics, nothing works for you. You must pass the two. With them, you will be able to speak the same money grammar and be able to add zeros in numbers because that is the rule. In all the topics taught in school in Mathematics, only tens were used. She didn't forget the unit and how to add zeroes to a figure. I don't know if we can remove this topic in Mathematics to build leaders who won't lead us to chaos.

A student in university is also expected to behave differently. He is a partial coach in his field but not complete coach because he is still learning. Some go to school because others go. Some go because they wanted to answer one of those that went. Some go because they want to belong to the school. Some go only to get a certificate and not to learn. Where do you belong?

Let's say you enter a new class. You ought to pass the exam of the old class to progress to the next. But if you don't pass out, you may not be promoted to the next class. When you pass it shows that you are merited and deserve to be in the next level. She got premature freedom. The colony gave this freedom to her. Not having the knowledge, it was premature freedom. Under the British, she was able to gather knowledge that she uses now. Some of the roads and bridges she uses now were built by the British. She forced the British to give her independence because she thinks that she had gotten some learned men who could takeover and the British gave in by giving her independence prematurely. Can one tree make a jungle? Make sure you give your children the answer to these questions.

She has universities built like the University of Nigeria Nsuka, which is supposed to be on par with the standard of Oxford, today. If that is true, why did these men send their children abroad to study? How many of those white men sent their kids to NSUKA University or any of the other Nigerian universities? If none, who is fooling who? How many of their children are studying in Nigeria's universities? See for yourself. How many of the American Presidents and British Prime Ministers and others study in Nigeria? A child that doesn't have television in his house goes outside to the neighbour's place to watch. If the child was insulted because of it and his father knows, his father would definitely be forced to buy a television. But if the child has a television set a home and it is not good or doesn't get the channels he wants, the child will go out. If the child has a satellite dish that brings all the channels, I believe that he will not be forced to go outside. Because Nigeria doesn't have good universities that's why her sons and daughters were sent abroad to study. She put the masses in the skull that she built and sends her children to school abroad! I am just saying what I saw.

The chicken says that the reason why it's crying is not that what is holding it will leave it but just for the world to hear its cries. As a citizen, you can rarely afford school fees. Their bills are like bombs. The school fee is like a national budget. If one sells his dog and buys a monkey, he still has a squatting animal in his house. You having this kind of university to confuse the world is hypocritical of the highest order.

If you give a child in primary school $2000 as his pocket money, what do you think he would ask on the first day? He would say: "This money is for me?" The cash is too much and will spoil the child. Do you know that it was an amount given to some officers as their monthly salary? Would a boy in primary school consume $2000 US dollar in a month? When you do this, you end up making the boy useless, telling him he doesn't need to put in efforts in life. The boy doesn't believe that you have to work to earn. He may not know that there are people who work for five months while some three years before they can lay their hands on such amounts. How would he know that if his parents don't help him know that? Giving the boy cash is not bad but giving him money to this extent is dangerous.

When an amount like this is given to him, he would recklessly use it, believing that his parents will send him more next month. This child will think that his dad will give him $5000 US dollar in his secondary school. If dad has the heart of giving him $5000 in his secondary school days, he will send him abroad with at least $10,000 as pocket money. What do you expect from the boy? He doesn't know what he can use that money for. He starts sponsoring cultism and armed robbery and might end up in trouble. How many succeeded in training their children in this manner?

19. THE POWER OF THE MIND!

Mind is the house where good and bad thoughts crop up. In a house, we have a kitchen where food is cooked. The mind can be said to be the kitchen of the body. The capacity of your mind is determined by the capacity it can contain. The capacity it can contain is determined by how far you can go, which is determined by how far you can reach. How far you can reach is your limit in life. Let me use this example: If you are not thinking of lakhs of rupees and abruptly you earn it, you may not know what to do with it. You are not thinking about cores of rupees but strangely you earn it, it can kill you or make you useless as in you may not have control of yourself. Your mind ought to be conquered first before the money comes. That is why you should maintain the habit of meditation. One day, I asked a boy, "If you are given a million dollars now, what would you use it for?" He replied that he didn't know what he could use it for because it was too much for him. Reading this now, you might say that the boy is stupid and you may wonder how he could he possibly say such nonsense. To you, it is nonsense, but he is sincere. Maybe, in his entire life, he hadn't thought of money. So what can be expected from him? For him to handle that much money, his mind must first handle it. Otherwise, he would be stupid and might not use it appropriately. Money is a spirit. Your mind has a lot of powers.

Power is the ability or capacity to do something or act in a particular way. It's what gives one energy to work or what produces the forces to work. The mind, the kitchen of the body if well-furnished, will have everything. If, for instance, you want to make your meal warm. But if you didn't know that your microwave could do this for you immediately, you may end up eating a cold meal. If you know how to use all those things in the kitchen you will be happy and won't find it difficult to cook anything.

Let's take the example of a little boy. Every day, his mother cooks for him and he goes to school. His mother works in the bank. One day, his mother forgot to fill his tiffin box. He came back from school famished. When he ransacked the kitchen, there was nothing to eat. He put on the gas and boiled white rice, added some pepper and salt. When the rice looked done partially, he ate it. Another day when he found nothing at home, he didn't know what to do. He opened the freezer and he saw fried chicken that his mother had kept in the fridge. He took it, with pepper, salt, and onions. He added oil. Without a recipe, he put all of it in the pot. It started boiling within a short while. When it was done, he ended up eating it, and fell into a stupor. He slept off till his mother came home. The aroma of the food met her nose. She wondered who had brought biryani home, because she knew she left home without any food. Without any question, she ate from the pot. She waited for a while and woke her son up, asking: "Who brought this dish for you?" Her son was shocked was scared that she might shout at him for taking all the ingredients that he did.

His mother asked again, "From which restaurant did you get this meal from? As I was eating it I nearly bit my finger because of the taste!"

Her son asked, "Mummy, really?"

"Yes!" she replied. "The restaurant you bought this from is super and they must be given an award for this!"

"An award?"

"Yes!"

"Then give it to me because I was the chef that made this!"

"You can't be serious! How did you do it?"

"Mummy, leave that! I think I can handle it. I was able to do this just because of difficulty in the moment of hunger."

Sometimes, difficulties can unleash your potentials. It can make you think of things that can help the world. It is from our mistakes that new products are made. Every new product comes from the mind.

Carl Benz and Henry Ford sat down in deep thought for years and came up with what the whole world is enjoying today. No matter how the present car manufacturers twist the car in the name of models, kudos still goes to the one whose thought was the power behind it. Two brothers used the power of their minds and made it possible to fly in the air and travel far and wide with the help of a plane!

When you think of an idea, it may seem stupid. But your mind is land owned only by you and nobody else. Only you have the right to build whatever you desire to build. If I tell you that there are so many things Carl Benz could have given the world if life had permitted him, you would say it's a lie. Maybe the state in which cars are today would have been different. Men took it from where he stopped and continued. Don't belittle yourself. An idle mind is the devil's workshop. The mind is an empty land indeed. Try filling the mind with something good, because anything can be prepared there, good and bad. Don't forget that there is nothing you cannot prepare in the kitchen. The mind is the only thing in the world that has so much volume as well as size. Try and develop it. Build something there before another builds something. It has to be occupied with something. Today there are men whose memory cannot be deleted from our minds. Why? Because of what their minds were able to bring out to make life more enjoyable today. They made great impacts in science with their inventions. Some of these people include:

William Caxton (1422–1491)

Not by virtue of the craft he fathered, nor for the practical success of the enterprise he boldly began, is the name of William Caxton honored by his countrymen. He was a successful merchant who upheld the good name of England abroad. He brought printing into England in the 15th Century. He was a patriotic, pious and cultured Englishman and printed by the same ideals as those by which he lived. He was not only the first printer, but one of the first educators, a molder of taste, and an establisher of literacy tradition.

Galileo Galilee (1564–1642)

He was one of the greatest of scientific pioneers. His name lives on as an astronomer who perfected the refracting telescope and showed men the heavens. But his support of the Copernican theory that the earth moved around the sun brought him under the anger of the church and darkened his life and achievements. His achievements in mechanics and dynamics were greater than his astronomical discoveries: he had a way of applying mathematical analysis to physical problems and in his work on the laws of motion he paved the way for Newton.

William Harvey (1578–1657)

There are some scientific phenomena with which we are so familiar, that it seems impossible that their truth could ever be doubted. It is incredible that only a few centuries divide us from the discoveries of the principles of gravity, solar motion and circulation of blood. When William Harvey put forward his theory of the circulation of blood in the body he shattered the medical beliefs of a thousand years and opened a new era of medical science.

John Flam steed (1646–1719)

"A prophet is not without honour, save in his own country." A few Englishmen today know or honor the name of John Flam steed. He was the father of modern astronomy, the first astronomer royal, who created all the astronomical tables in use in the 17th Century. He provided Newton with the observations that made the great man's discoveries possible. Racked with pain, handicapped by poverty, cramped and thwarted by his contemporaries, even by Newton himself, John Flam steed gave to the world in his life's work one of the greatest contributions to practical astronomy ever made by one man.

Sir Isaac Newton (1642–1727)

Our knowledge of the law of gravity, the principle by which the whole universe of sun, moon, earth and stars exist and move is due to Isaac Newton. To call him a great English mathematician is to let him down. At 24, he discovered the binomial theorem and the principles of integral calculus. Ten years before that, he was a farm boy with two years at a grammar school his credit! The invention of a reflecting telescope brought him to the notice of the Royal Society. Later, he was elected the President of the Royal Society for the last 25 years of his life. That and

Knighthood were the only tangible rewards given to one whose genius established for mankind "nature and nature's laws".

Luigi Galvani (1737–1798)

Who is not familiar with the theory of galvanism and with the galvanic battery? The word "galvanize" has become a semi-correct colloquialism. We regularly speak of a lethargic person, or body of persons, being galvanized into activity. Thousands use the word without thinking of Professor Luigi Galvani, of Bologna University, who first discovered the principle of animal electricity. He was the father of Galvanism. He was one of the pioneers of electrical science as we know it today. From the earliest times scientists have been trying to grasp, understand, harness and control electricity. His patient research, untiring work and brilliant discoveries led the world to our present age of electrical wonders. All of this has been the work of a continuous chain of seekers, carefully piecing their knowledge together to build a foundation for the seekers who came after. Through the years, from the days of Thales, we reap the fruits of the great minds of Galvani, who showed the way of Volta, of Franklin, Coulomb, Ousted, Henry and Davy, until we come to the mighty Faraday, who switched on the power for the modern world.

Michael Faraday (1791–1867)

Electricity has ceased to be an intangible phenomenon. It has become a domestic and industrial slave. Michael Faraday made this possible. His discovery of induced currents, which meant the production of electric current from magnetic force, was the dawn of a new epoch. He cleared the way for his followers to produce the dynamo, the generator of electric current. Indirectly, we owe it to him for electric light and power, the telephone telegraph, and a thousand other devices made possible by tapping electricity. On his work were based the research which led to the wireless telegraph. His experiments in electrolysis were invaluable. He magnetized light. He was a chemist and a physicist. A humble and brilliant scientist, his achievements are among the highest ever attained by humanity. Future research will tend not to dim nor diminish but to enhance and glorify the labours of this mighty investigator.

Alexander Graham Bell (1847–1922)

There is a monument to Alexander Graham Bell on almost every office desk: the telephone, it was fitting that this expert should discover the principle of the telephone and make the instrument by which nations may speak to nations. The revolution which the telephone has made in the life of the world is the measure of the gratitude we owe to him. By this great achievement, he stamped his name on the pages of history. "Mr. Watson, come here please, I want you." With these commonplace words a stocky, bearded Scotsman ushered in a new era. The speaker was Alexander Graham Bell and the sentence was the first to be spoken and received over a telephone. There is no need to expatiate on the importance of the telephone. It brought in the age of space-annihilation. No invention has surpassed it in usefulness. Today, we have millions of instruments, and the miracle of telephony has become commonplace in daily life.

Thomas Alva Edison (1847–1931)

Whenever you touch an electric switch or pick up the telephone, or turn the gramophone, or watch a film, you are paying an indirect tribute to the inventive and mechanical genius of Thomas Alva Edison. He had a way of making things work, of bringing things to pass and of overcoming obstacles thought to be insurmountable. His ingenuity and boldness were exactly the capabilities he needed, because he showed the way to profitable investments. He gave Bell's telephone a real transmitter and made it speak out loud and boldly. His name was placed on all of Bell's telephone sets. With his electromotograph, he furnished telegraphs with a new sounder, requiring neither a retractile spring to withdraw a mature from an electro-magnet nor any electro-magnet at all. He delivered the telegraph from the menace of Jay Gould, who controlled the patent on a retractile spring. Using the principle of this same electro-monograph, he provided a loud speaking receiver for the telephone. He established the fact that Bell's receiver was not indispensable any more than pages retractile spring was in telegraphy. Such a man naturally convinced financiers that he was handy to have around when they wished to escape suits for infringement and stake investments on schemes that were loosely to be "practical". He invented the phonograph. He was the first, to mechanically produce human speech and song. The phonograph aroused interest. Edison was looked upon as a wizard. To be applied to several practical uses, the phonograph had only to be developed. That development was postponed to make way for Edison's advance against a fresh impossibility - the subdivision of the electric current. From the invention issued the incandescent electric lamp, dynamos to supply it with a long series of auxiliary devices through which the centralization system of incandescent electric lighting was organized and rendered commercially possible.

Pierre and Marie quire (1859–1906, 1867–1934)

Scientific research into radioactivity after the discovery of radium opened eyes to a new world. In radium, they found themselves with an incalculably potent weapon for the war against diseases. The scientist that conferred this priceless gift on her fellow men was Marie Curie, who worked in conjunction with her husband. They first obtained radium from pitch blend, and then went on to discover its properties. The colossal value of her work is already apparent.

Orville and Wilbur Wright (1871–1912)

The aeroplane has ceased being a wonder to the world. Man's conquest of air travel has been so rapid that it came with a shock to realize that the first flight made by a machine heavier than air took place in 1903. Then, the possibility of an aeroplane was a distant dream. It became a reality through the vision, skill, courage and painstaking perseverance of two Americans, the Wright brothers, Orville and Wilbur Wright on December 17, 1903. To how many people is that a day of significance? It was a red letter day, celebrated throughout the world. On that day, was accomplished one of the most outstanding things in the history of mankind. A heavier than air flying machine came to be! True, the longest flight that day was but for 59 seconds and the distance was only 812 feet above ground. But man was about to realize an age old dream and emulate birds. Before this, men had flown in balloons. They had learned to glide and some even attempted heavier-than-air-flights, but no one succeeded.

These people can't be forgotten. LEARN TO MEDITATE. YOU HAVE A LOT TO CONTRIBUTE TO THE WORLD. DON'T FORGET THAT THE WORLD IS WAITING FOR YOU...

20. A COMPLAINANT

Don't be a complainant because a complainant admits failure. He always believes that he failed. He always cast blames and sticks to longer arguments that leads to fight. A complainant stresses issue and don't always agree. He wants everybody to pay attention to him always. He put to side issues that is to say he plays sides when it comes to matters arising. He is confusions. He likes gossip and always wants to listen to it because birds of the same feather flock together.

A complainant doesn't see any good about another. Because he was blind to see the good side he lays hold on the bad and complains. Yes because no one lies complain about the good deeds for him or towards him instead the bad deeds towards him. He talks in bitterness and always grumbles. He loves murmuring.

A lady came to me yesterday telling "Ogan I really need a good husband!" I asked her: "a good husband you say?" she replied "yes" she said all the men are like dogs. To get a good one is as difficult as eagle's egg. You can't trust men no matter what. They sleep around. They tell you this and they do that. Wow this is a nice poem you just sang now my dear. That means you have been observing them? I said answered "yes"! That means if your country makes you the chief security now I believe with this your observation character you possess now, nothing like crime huh? She boasts into laugh and said how? You just said now that you were looking for a good husband huh? And also you complimented the same group of men you want to be with that they are not trustworthy, that they couldn't be relied on. They are dogs and all men are the same. Look at all this were the compliments you rendered and yet you needed a good husband. By the way where will this good husband come from? I believe in the mist of those some men. Wow, why can't you see the good in them so as to make you own good to attract them? Do you know why they can't simply come to you because you complain a lot? Men hate complainants. I asked you again, a good husband you said huh? Firstly have you made yourself a good wife to be to attract them? See my dear, when you succeed in making yourself a good wife to be, you must definitely attract a good husband. She replied that she was trying her best to be a good wife to be but she doesn't know how to. Yes my dear, that you're I don't know how to has been what is keeping the good one not to come. You don't need to search for a good husband first make yourself a good wife to be a good husband will search for you. Good wives are not found everywhere because they are always hidden. I didn't say that you should go and hide yourself ooh? They are sorted out with touch light. A good wife is not in the beauty or money but in the character. You should know that the worst thing that can happen to a man is when he marries a bag wife. If he does, he is finished. Lady Holland says: "Troubles like babies grow larger by nursing."

Come on my dear complaining is never and not an answer to our challenges in life. Have a positive mental attitude is everything. Charles Dickens says "Reflect upon your present blessings, of which every man has plenty; not on your past misfortunes, of which all men have some. How do you feel when people come around you and put down all of their challenges and complain to you? Really it doesn't lift your spirit is it not? You know one thing about life we live; nobody wants to be close to a complainant. I know that we all complain in one way or the other. As yourself how often do you really complain? If you want to know whether you complain as that fellow close to you. Sharing your experiences and disappointments with friends or family members in the context of having them up to date on the latest development in your life is out of what we are talking about. After all bible records that we should give teaming that is to say testify lords doing in your life and it didn't say complain the lords doing in your life. Part of being human is sharing our expenses and supporting each other. Do you think anybody wants to listen to your pains? Earl Nightingale says "self-pity is an acid which eats holes in happiness." When you got a pain, realize how fortunate you are. Face the rest of the day with good attitude otherwise I say better attitude. Renew your energy in you see that you will feel better instead of complaining. I use to have a teacher, when he gets angry or when men provokes him, instead of reacting, or fighting because he knew that he is a boxer. If he eventually loses his mind it will result to killing someone. What does he do in this case? He goes to the pitch and start pouring the anger on a bag of sand by hitting it hardly. William Penn says "the secret of happiness is to count your blessings while others are adding up their troubles.

What I am putting across to you is however, rather than putting complains it's better to keep your eyes on those steps it will take you to solve or conquer so as to lessen your burden. Let's assume you are feeling a little tired of recently. Instead of you to be telling everyone how lousy you feel, make an effort to exercise more regularly or get to bed a little earlier.

If your conversation is full of complain the second person get bored. People who don't complain too much and those who uplift your spirit in your conversation as in speak positive words are a joy to be around. Make up your mind to join these men otherwise people will have no other choice than to cross the secret when you are coming or when they see you coming.

21. OBSERVE A CHANGE

So many people complain when the face differs situations and would even say words that are not consistence with what God says about them and whereby putting their lives in jeopardy because of what they say with their mouth. Don't forget in our previous topic which says and also was pointing to the power of spoken words. That whatever thing you say with your mouth that I will do. God wasn't making a mistake when he was saying or making those statements. Mind you He is still God He doesn't make mistakes and never late.

Now observe a change. When a change comes it comes with divers challenges which sometime when you see the challenge you will not take cognizance of the change it wants to bring. And might be misinterpreted by you whereby leading you in the part of chaos and left you in the house of regret.

Take for instance human nature. When a woman didn't see her period, when she faces some unkind or unusual sickness and also vomiting, it is a challenge that will lead to bringing forth a new human being into the world. When a baby wants to grow teeth. It falls ill as many times as it could and it could lead to be visiting the doctor often and on. Take a look, at a young growing girl that often takes her bath outside or in a public place, one she or he observes the change in her body, nobody will tell her to stop taking bath outside again immediately the change comes, she will be conscious of her body now always wearing her towel so that nobody would see her body again somebody she doesn't care if anybody was looking at previously.

Another one that looks like it again is when the weather changes it also brings a change only just observe it and the change it's coming with. Have you taken notice of this that every time we have change of weather people fall sick here and there you begin to see almost everyone coughing as a result they visit the doctor in the hospital? And they also spend money. In women for this change to come; she must see her monthly period that is the sign of change of a full womanhood. Just observe the change.

Something happened one day. Don't forget observe the change whenever it wants to come. Admit that this is for a change and its bringing goodies to you. Bible records that everything works for good for those that loves God. It didn't say something are working for good or those ones you liked would work for good but everything just to bring a new change. Observe the change so that you will not lament when the breeze of change comes. A lady Priya was dating a guy by name wool for five years and the guy promised her marriage and both of them continued to date not until one day she happens to introduce her fellow girl by name Lucia to her boyfriend wool whom she told a lot about and that they were getting married as soon as possible. During these five years of their date, she never knew that the guy in question was an armed robber. One day her so called girlfriend that she introduced to her boyfriend went at her back backbiting that she was this and that and her guy left if not using the word abounded her for her girl friend who told the tale to him. As he abounded his first love for her close friend both began to do things together and finally got married after four months of knowing each other. Now his first love that he dumped stayed indoors and cried many days.

The question is

Why would this girl cry for this long time? Why? The reason is that she never understood the reason why that happened was for a reason and that reason is for a change in her life. God really want to fix her where she belong and for that to happen, there is always challenging in the middle of every change don't forget that. As God may have it, one of the governors of the state happen to meet her in the occasion she was fortunate to attend and the governor told her that he would love to marry her in fact the whole story in there was that he proposed to her even without any dating. And the both finally got married. After three years, they came to reality. She was having a baby girl and was also pregnant for another baby. What really happened to her girlfriend: who took away her man from her? Look at the way nature does its own activities. Now Lucia was having two kids for that Mr. Wool. Just few years later, the news was that wool was shut down dead on the highway robbing people. Wow nature and change now the wife Lucia was left with nothing but the same tears she left on the eyes of her friend Priya her close friend by taking her pains away indirectly. You see by snatching Wool from Priya, Lucia now took away her worries because Lucia must definitely be a widow now. The widow Priya had become in ignorance she doesn't know. Even if a prophet had told her she wouldn't believe her eyes. Someday are like that.

Observe the change when it comes because it comes with some challenges something that leads to tears if you didn't observe it that it was for a change.

Now let's drive it down to our daily activities. Before we proceed, you should remember that before is Israelites exudes to the cannon land, there was a change. Those that didn't observe the change were busy arguing and never left with them. Never knew it was for a change.

Even as at that change you know comes with suffering sometimes. So those that did observe that change didn't go with them to cannon land, when the suffering that follows the change came. So many of them said words that are not consistence with the plans God had for them. Because God wants to give cannon to Israelite that was the reason of allowing them to drink from the cup of suffering in the land of Egypt. That cup of suffering they observed in Egypt was for the change.

Jesus is a good example for a change. He decided to give his life for us so that we may obtain peace and eternal life. Those precious scarifies was for a change for us to be saved. Having being aware of the glory; the crown awaiting Him, He endured the suffering to the end... The suffering could be called the suffering on the cross which brought to us is salvation.

For you to know and also appreciate gold it must observe a change. How do I mean by observing a change? The gold must be melted for it to be in the shape you want it to be. For gold to be melted so that you will be able to mould anything you wish to mould with it, it must suffer the heat in the fire that is furnace of fire. I wish you understand the degree of fire it must be in before the change will come. It is that fire that that makes it the most admirable treasure and more also costly. How do you see it??

Many at times things happen we don't seem to observe that it's for a change. One man was sent to jail on false accusation you may say without committing any crime and was suffering and suffering of which nobody was coming for him to see to his case in there. But afterwards he became a king in that land. How did it happen otherwise you may say how possible is it? He got the contact that made him a king from that jail. Jail was an opportunity for him to become a king. If he was outside in the free air marrying he may not have the opportunity of becoming a kind because he was nobody to meet with or come close to the king's palace. But inside the jail you meet assorted timber and alibis which ordinarily in the free air you couldn't come close to them. What made this young fellow to enter inside the jail was because of the offence another fellow committed and he was replaced for the guy and was presented to the court that was the one. When the suffering was too much in the jail no good food no good accommodation and he nearly committed suicide. But as God may have it he was saved in the jail there. It was at the process of trying to committee suicide the contract with the man that made him the king came to be. Had it been that he committed suicide and died without observing that it was for a change of status, that God threw him in there (jail). If he hadn't gone in there, he wouldn't have met that fellow talk more of becoming the king. To him now that jail was one opportunity for him to become a king but never said you should go and commit crime so that you will enter inside of the jail to become a king. Mind you that every suffering calls for a change either negative or positive.

In the chemistry there is what science called change. In this change there is physical change and chemical change. Physical change is reversible and no new substance is found and chemical change is not reversible and new substance is found. In the process of a change something must happen don't forget that.

When something happens in your life don't cast blames, just see the change it was to bring and crab it to becoming and moving to the next post office God had placed you.

Observe a change my dear it's very important. It is for a promotion. The lesson I want to put across is that you shouldn't complain but observe that what happened was for a change. And the change is for your promotion. It also means that every change cost you something either pains or finance or both at the same time.

22. A WINNER

WHO IS A WINNER?

A winner is the last man standing. It takes a great heart to win. Do you know why it is so? Because winners never quit and quitters never win! He that fights and run away doesn't win but out of fear, he flew. Don't forget that when you flew or run away you will still come back to meet the unforgotten fight. A winner can spend his last blood to the end of the fight just because he wants to win for the trophy is waiting for X winners!!! A winner doesn't look at the fight rather he focuses on the trophy. A winner doesn't just win because he wants to win but he always prepared to win in his mind then helps himself with the physical preparations. A winner has the mentality of it's not over until it's all over. This means that he fights till the last second of the fight because it takes a second to win. He has it that the next move is always dangerous 'because it takes the next step to win. He doesn't take a chance. A winner takes advantage of every opportunity. A winner doesn't play with his mother SUCCESS!!!

23. A GOOD OBSERVER

1. A good observer is a watchman; He is always focused on his gaze.
2. A good observer is a person who looks with proper scrutiny.
3. A good observer is a person who looks with carefulness.
4. A good observer is a person who believes in absolute serenity and tranquillity.
5. A good observer is a person who doesn't lose concentration.
6. A good observer is a person doesn't permit distraction. He stays at focal points.
7. A good observer is a person that studies the mind first.
8. A good observer doesn't talk much instead he watches and listens not sometimes but all the time.
9. A good observer doesn't need crowd when he pins his attention on what he is observing because crowd causes distraction. If you want to avoid distraction, you must avoid crowd.
10. A good observer monitors and memorizes whatever thing that is going on around at any given time.
11. A good observer knows the law. He is always at alert.
12. A good observer always gathers information for reference purposes.
13. A good observer easily dictates spy in the mist.
14. A good observer reads meaning in every word thrown out as a statement.
15. A good observer is a watchman; He is always focused on his gaze.
16. A good observer is a person who looks with proper scrutiny.
17. A good observer is a person who looks with carefulness.
18. A good observer is a person who believes in absolute serenity and tranquility.
19. A good observer is a person who doesn't lose concentration.
20. A good observer is a person doesn't permit distraction. He stays at focal points.

21. A good observer is a person that studies the mind first.
22. A good observer doesn't talk much instead he watches and listens not sometimes but all the time.
23. A good observer doesn't need crowd when he pins his attention on what he is observing because crowd causes distraction. If you want to avoid distraction, you must avoid crowd.
24. A good observer monitors and memorizes whatever thing that is going on around at any given time.
25. A good observer knows the law. He is always at alert.
26. A good observer always gathers information for reference purposes.
27. A good observer easily dictates spy in the mist.
28. A good observer reads meaning in every word thrown out as a statement.

24. DON'T BE GREEDY

Greedy is having a selfish desire to have more of something (such as money or food) very eager to. Greedy carries wickedness in disguise. There is no greedy that doesn't have an act of wickedness at the back. A man who is greedy is ready to kill. A man who is greedy is covetous because he thinks that success lies on the abundance of the things he possesses. Take a look at the bible where it records in (Luke 12v15) NKJV). And he said to them, "Take need and beware of covetousness, for one's life does not consist in the abundance of the things he possesses.

A greedy man thinks that success is measured according to what you possess in the sight of god that is why he is not contented with the one he had. Bible didn't say you shouldn't hunger for increase but not in greed manners.

A greedy man never sat down to ask what true success really is or what the symbols of true success are how doing you measure success? Do you use the symbols of the world to tell whether you're successful or not? A greedy man thinks that success is all about making more money or having more influence in the money or having more successful because you are widely known and maybe celebrated by men or because you have this world goods.

True success transcends all of these. True success is being the man or woman god has called you to be and fulfilling his call on your life no matter what the people around think. Whether or not you have the world's symbols of success it's unimportant. A greedy man does not know that true success is to be what god called you to be because he made you. He's the only one who knows the reason you're in this world check the bible in (1 peter 2:9).

If a car manufacturer puts a car on the road and the car functions according to the manufacturer's specifications then it is said to be successful. But it is only a greedy man who would like to change the manufacturer's specifications to his specification. How? A car is made to carry four passengers on board but it is only a greedy man who will be using that same car that was made for four passengers to carry seven passengers with a lot of load. What do you think that will happen to the car?

Don't be greedy. Don't miss use life! Be who god had called you to be and do what he called you to do anything else is insignificant. What counts is to be a success with God. God hates a greedy man.

25. CAN YOU STOP CRIME?

First what is crime?

Crime is just going contradictory to the ruling authority to presently accepted norms traditions or culture. When we say crime, we talk about going against the law.

In the olden days: there are some things we do you would be punished otherwise banish from the village. During those period of time, lesbianism and homosexuals is something when you try it, definitely you would be killed. Prostitution was not rampant and chastity was maintained by women. Bribery and corruption was on a low key but today it's been modernized. Tradition and law was maintained and justice prevailed but today the so called justice is for the rich and renounced personnel's. The so called law was made for the poor not the rich.

Can you really stop crime was the question? If you would venture, in which way do you think you would? How do you start and where do you start from? You can't stop crime instead you look for a way to minimize it. Let me ask you my dear crime stopper, how you stop crime when people who are at the top create crime themselves! Or don't you know that you could create an avenue for crime? Let's go down a bit and see how it goes.

Lecturers who supposed to join in fighting crime are purposely failing the students just because he wants to either collect money from the boys or sleep with the girls as his concubines. During the entrance exams, students that get merit had been denied admission because they didn't give bribe to the lecturer. A student graduated but to collect his certificate is a big challenge for him because the fee just to collect that certificate is like a national budget. If this could happen in school of learning where you should learn morals, where else is save? I believe that the leaders that are leading us passed through this orientation of priory and corruption that means they would be corrupted more than the lecturers in future.

The government told us that police is our friend. Wow! That's sounds interesting. With little experience I had I don't think that statement was truth. How do we really believe that? Let me tell you my dear friend:

When MR CORRUCTION gets married to MISS CRIME they give birth to PROF. CRIMINAL.

If MR DOCTOR eventually marries a MISS NURSE they will give birth to a patient.

If SIR POLICE marries a HON. MISS LAWYER, they give birth to a SIR JAIL WARDER.

Imagine in a world of ours where everything is upside down. Where Mr. CORRUPTION is busy asking PROF. CRIMINAL why he is committing CRIME? Are you shocked? Don't be because I am going to tell you more about MR CORRUPTION and PROFF. CRIMINAL.

The question is: why are we deceiving ourselves? Yes, it was true that the police men were doing their duty punishing the people that committed Madam Crime but why do you take laws into your hands Mr. Police by beating that fellow? You were beating and molesting these fellows in the name that they were suspects. The question is who is suspecting you when you take brides? Anyways it's never your fault because Mr. Government licensed you to do crime without any quires. Like father like some. The lecturer who lectured you is also a robber in his own pattern and you doing the same thing no stress huh. You are busy beating these fellow because you feel that Mr. Government gave you license to do so and you forget that it is not good for a thief to punish a thief. Why should you when what you were beating them for you are also a culprit. I think this is stupid. We know that all goats eat shit but it's the one that we see carrying shit on its teeth we pursue. In this case you are right but don't forget you eat the same shit.

Just like when mom will see or catches her daughter making love with her lover and she starts beating her, is it good for that kind of mom to be seen messing around with men let alone heaving it as a rumour? But do you know even as a mummy finished beating her daughter for having sex with her boyfriend yet the same night mom left her boyfriend's house. How does it sound? Because she was not caught once now she stands a good mother to beat that girl who happens to be her daughter in the name of training or making her to be a good citizen. Even if nobody had caught her but her conscience will always say my dear you are guilty of what you are beating that girl of. No regarding making love, I want you to know that if finally she was caught red handed doing the same thing which she was beating her daughter for may be by the husband what kind of eye do you think that her daughter would seeing her with? We are living in the era of thief punishing chief! It is just like born thief verses unborn chief! This one's skirt had been opened for the world to see her anus. That your anus is covered with your something for now but for how long is the question?

A police man who claims to be doing his duty can decide to move against an innocent fellows and snatch their money in the name of arrest because Mr. government gave him license to do so and they would say to you indirectly don't expose them for whatever thing you say would be hold against you in the law court. They would use grammar to intimidate you when they had collected anything called cash with you. If you talk, they put another case on your head. What will you do then? They are to give report not you. Where do you see human right? Thief on a duty post waiting for a fellow thief maybe they didn't give them their own share. What are you really doing on that check point? Who are you checking? Your fellow thief on duty? Why do you stand there as if you are a good? Why do you make out as if you don't eat meat when you use your teeth to share it for the kids? A star that ought to be followed after is now going to some idiotic places knowing full well that whether by omission or commission he must be seen. You should know that nothing is hidden under the sun. A big fish doesn't have a hiding place in the sea.

Imagine a police man telling a robber: "you robber, you said you were not going to give me my own share, don't worry you are going to jail. Robber asked the police man if he was threading him with the word jail? The policeman said to the robber: "I will make sure I use my office to put you in prison. Wow the robber said so you guys are using your offices to jail people and nobody had ever jailed you huh? Robber said to the police man: "Do you see what Mr. Government is doing committing crime by licensing group of robber in a uniform to rob people in the name of police huh? The robber started shading tears saying: "My fellow robber in uniform why do you treat us like this as if we are not fellow brothers in crime? Don't forget that if we robbers are to be nailed or sentenced don't forget that yours is afterwards. The police man said to the robbers: what do you mean by that?" Robber said: why do you address us as just robbers instead of calling us or using the word "my fellow robbers?" what is your problem Mr. Police office? As they were dragging the issue, the governor that they went to rob in his house now dash in and said: "where are those robbers? Immediately they were brought to him and threw governor said" you people had the impetus to come to my house and rob me eh? One of robbers replied saying: "Mr. governor, with dual respect, it's not that we had the heart to rob you but it's just that we decided to visit our fellow robbers house since he does not want to invoice us officially to work. And since our fellow robber had the heart of robbing a whole state, after all how much did we collect from you? Just $20,000,000 twenty million dollars and you are here shouting and ranting when you have been busy robbing our state of billions dollars per second billing direct and indirect and have chances of getting more of this billions till you come down from the seat and we only collect just $20,000,000 twenty million dollars from you on a one strike of which we don't know when we will get another one besides we were just five guys here to share this cash and you are just only you for the whole of those billions. Governor said: "okay, agreed but why do you shout my wife and reap my daughter? Robbers said: "Mr. Governor, we have reasons of shutting your wife and reaping your daughter. We know that she is your only daughter that was why we did it. Mr. Governor said. "You guys are very wicked how could you do such a thing?" Robbers said Mr. Governor; we did it because we just want to make sure that you feel our pains. As for shutting your wife, she was dragging the money with us, she never gave room for us to carry the little cash and go when she knows that you the husband are also a robber robbing a whole state and she doesn't want to let go that small amount. She knows that; that particular amount she could spend it in just one month. We saw the greed in her eyes and we decided to shut aside. Governor said: "how could you say I your governor that governs your state is a robber? Robber said: "your excellence sir, you are speaking English. Try to understand that big fish doesn't have a hidden place. Don't you know that the 20 billion dollars you smuggled to France last week was our man who did it for you? Don't you know that the refinery you suppose to build here for us at least lessen unemployment which you build in South Africa and sometime we are aware of everything? The hospital you supposed to build here for us you went and built it in South Africa and it was said to be the best hospital in all the hospital there. Now you had flew you wife abroad because your mind had condemned you that the low facilities and poor support you gave to our indigenous doctors had given you a failing heart that they could kill your wife huh? Don't you know that I am an engineer a petro chin engineer for that matter? Don't you know that the refinery you built in satiate if it was to be built or fixed in here; you would have given me chance of practicing my course in school? Put smile on my face and remove greed and the spirit of what was caught doing. The guy that shut your wife in particular is a doctor do you know? If that hospital was here you built it you will not rush your wife to abroad because I believe that Dr. Mica would have taken care of her as her excellence she is. I don't want to say what you are using the cash you were dumping in Switzerland to do. I need to take care of my family. My last sister had been studying for six years now for a course of three years. The question is why? Because member (1) she refused to sleep with her lecture and he kept on failing her like he promised.

(2) Because you refused to pay the lectures and they kept on going on strike because they couldn't beat you or do you anything. You were complaining that we reaped your only daughter huh? You're never wanted your daughter to experience what my own sister was passing through then you flew her to abroad. You knew you put no facilities and you had transferred the salary of the lectures to France and Switzerland in your account. Some of the schools, no teachers. But you needed good and quality education for your darling only daughter huh that was why you sent abroad to go and study and your idiots who couldn't afford to sponsor theirs abroad should either attend this or they leave. Because some teachers were angry foe not being paid and some of them lives on the students. If the students didn't co-operate, she fails in

her exams. If a student didn't open her legs she will study for 2 years extra. The money that you would have used to make the teachers happy and refuse their minds from these idiotic activities you packed them dumped them somewhere to be idle cash. All of them just for this your daughter or whose? Now you have seen the reason why I called you my fellow robber his Excellency (governor) whenever I called you my fellow robber I believe you should answer me in fact my fellow bigger robber. In our tradition Mr. governor, when one sees his elder brother, he should recognize him by calling him big bros so that's the reason I called you my fellow bigger robber because the money you are robbing is too much. Permit me to respect you by calling you my fellow bigger robber. What are you doing with those cash you are dumping abroad? You are dumping it out of wickedness if not, how many are you in your family that they can't use one hundred million dollar to establish but you confiscated more than $30,000,000,000 thirty billion dollars to the detriment of the poor masses. Now you those cash idol and jobless. I wonder why someone would keep like one hundred thousand bags of rice for only his family even if they are hundred in that house when he knows that he could always buy fresh from the market. This could be called stupidity to the highest order. You were busy speaking big grammar because you know that a lie is good in spoken grammar. My fellow big robber, I want to ask oooh, every month you push out 1 million dollars from the location then if eventually Obama or the queen Elizabeth visits, it becomes an avenue to Transat some money as business not even some but almost all the money. I was wondering if what you specialized in your course in college if it was transfer? When queen visits, you told us that you used $1,000,000 (one million dollars) for her tea and $2,000,000 (two million dollars) for her hotel and $5,000,000 (five million dollars) for entertainment then another $5,000,000 (five million dollars) for her flight back to UK imagine. My fellow bigger robber (no be like that nee). Queen Elizabeth ma, I don't know that you were such a fact woman this one my fellow bigger robber is using the kind of money that we could use to build atheist confirmed three star hotel to lodge you in a room. I am beginning to think that the room must be as big as a whole hotel. Yes it is true. For your flight, my fellow bigger robber is buying a brand new jet for you flight ticket? For you tea, my fellow bigger robber opened a coffee farm on your head in the name of tea. Ooh my God, God please I want to taste this kind of tea I believe anyone that takes this kind of tea that you used $1,000,000 (one million dollars) to do will not die again. God, I plead with you if only you would allow me to taste this $1,000,000 (one million dollars) tea I will be grateful. God see I am not greedy like my fellow bigger robber who wants to drink the whole cup. I really want to taste this tea not the full cup.

You have not less than 50 private cars lying low in your compound doing nothing yet some people working under you go on ten toes. How do you expect us to be happy?

You asked before reasons why we raped your only daughter right? I believe I never gave you an enough reasons but the answer is not far-fetched you know why? Although the girl was innocent for us to act that kind of thing upon but I didn't forget that my own sweet sister was innocent for to act that kind of things upon but I didn't forget that my sweet sister was harassed sexually for taking money from a so called sugar daddy like you because she wanted to meet up her school fees. I believed that this daughter never did this kind of rubbish just to meet up? If I may ask, what exactly does she want to meet up for when you kept all the token money for her? The money you would have used to pay my dad when he was alive was transferred by you to an unknown land called abroad. Was it not an act of wickedness? Now you are not happy because it affected you. It is your daughter that is why you were shouting and ranting then did you think of other people's daughter? You really want to tell us that your daughter is Miss World huh? And other people's daughters are Miss local right? Who wants to die in lie if I may ask? I believe nobody and that is why everybody is fighting tooth and nail to become a good robber. Yes a good robber. Don't misconstrue me on the world I used (a good robber) governor asked, now what do you want? Robber says: "our fellow bigger robber, settle the masses and stop this jungle bell preaching. Settle the masses, how? Governor ask: robbers said: "make availability of those things that warranted some of this idiotic activities in the town to be minimized because I know you can't stop crime but at least to a minimum rate. Otherwise of it you will face more of this. After all if you were doing well, you would have the opportunity to seat with us the way you just did now because you were afraid of what you were doing you choose to be on convoy abed 50 police men at the same time so that we can see you and talk to you. "When someone's corpse is being carried it looks as if it was just more fire wood." It was because we wanted to collect our share from the cake that belongs to all of us that you were eating alone so don't use jail to threaten us because I know that before you finish this tenor, you are going to be probed and you are coming in with us whether you like it or not. It is not only you but with all the fellow bigger robbers, that surrounded you both big and small. Governor said how? Please tell me who are those robbers you know?

Robbers say: "is it because they are not carrying guns? Don't mind some are robbing with another different AK47. We often call it during the school days (chain bullet pistol) wow I believe you've not heard about it once? This particular gun kills more than (gerent bomb) governor said: are you sure of what you were saying because I have metal dictating everywhere around me it can dictate guns easily. Imagine a metal dictator. Please don't make out new as if you don't know. Governor said really, I don't know. If I know those people definitely they must join you to jail. The robbers boost into laugh my fellow big robber; all you cabinets including you are using this almighty chain bullet pistol. Governor, if I may ask, when you see or catch someone with the pistol will he also go to jail? Governor rush the answer and said of course yes that means you have to come in with us now. Governor said how? Robbers replied, my fellow big robber you are now caught red handed with the pistol on your chest. Where is it? Asked the governor. That pen you are having there is the chain bullet pistol I am talking about which you have been using to lurk all the cash of the general citizenry. You have been robbing us and claim to be doing your duty. That pen you are having is the one we called the almighty AK56. Governor fainted! You use this pen to sign death warrant of so many men who never supported your robbing. You use it to add beautiful zeros to some figures and we use AK47 to sign this small 20 million dollar which you know that it was for 5 of us here yet you are getting greedy mind. If you say that you are not greedy, why do you order for our arrest? See our fellow bigger robber; there are many types of stealing ooh. Sorry for using the word stealing permitted me to use the word robber I hope it would be okay for you? Now we say:

TYPES OF ROBBING

- Office robbing
- High way robbing
- House robbing
- School robbing
- Police robbing (intimidation)
- Market robbing
- Authority robbing
- Sex robbing (raping)
- Picking pockets
- Brain robbing (internet fraud)

Note: whether you put the rope to someone's head or someone's head to the rope both are hanging. The rope is just on the neck.

You can't separate the rope from the head neither will you separate the head from the rope. I want to make you to understand that robbing is robbing whether you term it stealing or baptize it thieving pocketing picking or obtaining or luring or money laundry or outsmarting, talking or tricking after gathering all this names in the name of grammar believe me all are same. The baptismal names are all those I mentioned but the surname that joins all of them is robbing. You can rob with hand, you can rob with pen which is the most dangerous because this particular robbing can rob off $100,000,000 (one trillion dollars) without you knowing let alone arresting him with a dim if not seeing the pen only.

Robbing done with pen is one of the big boy's robbing. On like what we were discussing about types of robbing,

OFFICE ROBBING: these are the robbing done in the offices. How do I mean will be your question now? Yes when you come to offices, so many activities are going on. The removed the name robbing and baptized it RACKETING. Imagine the sweet word RACKETING. Wow. This is camouflage. A criminal vocabulary. E.g. a particular project was issued out for the benefit of the masses now it starts from our fellow bigger robber his Excellency governor; you make or signed a magnitude of contract worth $50,000,000,000. 50 billion dollars for road construction. A road even the poor masses know that shouldn't take up to $30,000,000. 30 million dollars even if it takes up to that $50,000,000,000. 50 billion dollars mentioned that means the road must be above high quality. More standardized than what we thought it would be. No because you are the one on seat of authority, you immediately take advantage of your authority that even if you shot all the whole money with your pen nothing will happen and nobody will query you either. This is what I called AUTHORITY ROBBING.

You use your mathematical skills to add beautiful zeros because you know very well that one zero is very dangerous and disastrous in a figure. You know full well that one zero can remove raised to power ten of what you thought in a figure.

The AUTHORITY ROBBERS are the only robbers that know the value of MR. ZERO in a figure. Once they want to start, they cock their chain bullet pistol which everybody knows as (MR PEN) to shooting all the money available... GIGIGIGIGII will be the sound you will hear nonstop because he knows that the so called bullet that he is using to shot is not costly (ink).

The contract is $50,000,000, (fifty million dollars) but you had used you pistol to add just one zero wow. For those whose doesn't know the power of zero? This is $50,000,000 once you add just one zero now has it become five hundred million 50,000,000 + 0 = $500,000,000 wonderful. The power of MR ZERO in a figure!

Of which when you subtract 50,000,000dollars from the 500,000,000dollars you have left over 450,000,000 dollars just like that. That's interesting. This is real confirmed robbing in a smarter manner. Yet your stupid conscience allowed you to talk about crime? The worse is that you don't have shame to talk on front of the citizenry. But my fellow bigger robber, do you know that the people you are robbing are masses?

My God! Mr. President came for visiting in your state then you turn it to means of robbing the money that belongs to the state.

You told us on television that you used $100,000dollars to buy the water that you gave Mr. President to drink for the visit. Wow that's nice. That sounds reasonable huh. Sorry Mr. President you must be a bull we use in the farm that drinks one drum of water before the day passes. Even if you are not a bull in the form to drink water worth of $100,000 but my fellow bigger robber is here indirectly calling you a bull! Otherwise you work like a bull in the farm when you seat on AC chair, sleep in an AC room, bath in an AC bathroom excrete in an AC toilet, enter in an AC car work in an AC office.

I wonder when last you enter or feel the sun and my fellow bigger robber is busy calling you a bull that drinks $100,000 water per day.

After hearing this and you leave him to embezzle that money that is when I will believe you were the bull that he called you.

Remember that the masses know how much EVA mineral water cost in the market. They know how much it is been sold! Why I am saying this is that if my fellow robber Mr. governor says that he used 100,000 $ in a restaurant that food is more costly than water even costlier I believe that what you are paying for is the food and not the water.

This means you Mr. President didn't go back hungry or in hunger you must have taking some food at least cake. Even as eat when we were watching Mr. President Visit we never saw him ate rice or kpomo rather some cake and coffee. Now my fellow bigger robber told us that he used $ 1,000,000 one million dollars for water on a visit not a stay which means that you must be spending around $5,000,000 five million dollars for water as Mr. President you are. I believe that someone who uses $1,000,000 one million dollars for drinking water in a day of which Mr. president never sat down for more than 3 hrs just to give speech and go is capable of building or having like 30–40 big international standard companies around where his citizens are working and getting their own cash for their drinking water.

If my fellow bigger robber could give Mr. President water worth that kind of amount which must be heavenly water I wonder what will happens and how many trillions that will be used to give Mr. president water when he stay for a year. It means that our country is loaded. We are loaded financially yet the citizens are suffering. Just check 1,000,000 x 30 days of the month = 30,000,000 $ wow wonderful. For a year would be 30,000,000 x 12 = 300,000,000 $ for water alone in a year. This is too much Mr. President. You must be the bull he called you indirectly. If he could spend such an amount for this water that means that the major thing that he would put money would be superb I am referring to our fellow bigger robber (governor).

He told us that in health sector agricultural sector, 30 billion $ sports will be $12,000,000 (twelve billion dollars) $200,000,000 (two hundred billion dollar) I remembered what he did when he was constructing that shot road he told us $50,000,000 fifty million dollars which was changed to $500,000,000 (five hundred million), now this one is assumed 500 billion $, he may cold one zero which you know if he does, the whole money would have finished. 500,000,000,000 + 0 = 5,000,000,000,000 = $5 trillion Wahoo. If this happens we must be in debt FOREVER just because of one person the whole state is in debt. What power of ZERO.

This is why they will say that they want to privatize all sectors like power, oil refinery etc. They will privatize the oil sector and they will be the one to buy it.

He will tell you that even the sea woof needs privatization so as to make it work then he will declare it for sell and use our money to buying it. Imagine it now remains for my fellow bigger robber to declare the whole state for sale and also buys it.

God are you there with your two eyes open seeing all this atrocities? I see that the joke is funny huh?

Thanks for enjoying it but you know that there is truth in what I was saying.

What a joke from a true story.

Believe me OFFICE ROBBING is highly technical. In a state that such cash is being spent for all these yet the citizenry are hungry. Even if this state are up to 1 million people and a billion $ is shared among her citizenry don't you think that each citizen will be riding a jeep? They also would get good amount every month for their up keep. But my fellow bigger robber will say no to this regard and will love to transfer all the funds to foreign accounts and make the whole cash idol and jobless.

He just wants to prove to the public that he studied transferology if there is any course like that in the university.

School Robbing

The lecturers who we look up to are agitating on how to stop crime. How do you use demon to cheese a demon? You can imagine that a whole lecturer whom we are looking up to is also a cultist? Wow now you really want to stop cultism in the college? No way. Lecturers now turn their female students to female dogs just to satisfy their sexual feelings. He turns his male students to armed robbers and female wide harlots.

I see you are looking at me now. I think before you talk about stopping crime you should first stop the crime in you. EVERYBODY WANTS A CHANGE BUT NONE WANTS TO BE CHANGED... who is to be blamed?

I expect how in your return question. Before you get admission into university so called, the orientation is getting ready to flow with the flow. Where do they want you to flow? Flowing on top of corruption. Yes the first course you will learn is PROSTITUTION 101 as a female undermining the age. It is called: sleep with me and have Alpha in my course.

If you agree, go and book a hotel then tomorrow open it for me. Hey, open what sir? Is that a question? Anyway if you don't understand what that word open means ask your female friends or wait until you fail you will know how far.

So you mean you don't understand then write on the quiz sheet; I don't understand sir okay.

Some lecturers had turned their offices to MOONSHINE HOTELS where they sleep almost all the female students in the campus.

Look at it and don't make out now as if you don't know otherwise set a trap you will catch a meet:

Cynthia look at you. You didn't even take the exam but you had 'A' Alpha?

Chioma didn't write anything yet she got "A" Alpha.

This must be magic or something else. My dear it's not magic or something else it's the power of what we called button power. Tomorrow Cynthia will confidently tell you that if you like read all the topics that she is going to club and definitely will pass the exam.

What do you think that gave her the confidence? Because she didn't forget the orientation of FLOW WITH THE FLOW AND SUCCEED.

Look at Mr. Lecturer is busy looking at me now as if all I said was an accusation when he knew it was a full grown truth.

Please stop looking at me like that. Am I talking about this when Florence and Sandra had booked already CITIZEN HOTEL room 202 against tomorrow for your SHAMEFUL ACT?

Please stop looking at me. Now you graduated her with a good result as a medical doctor and gave her license to kill people the way she wants as a doctor.

Please my dear, don't go to her hospital ooh if you want to be alive. Otherwise she will kill you not even mare mistake but intentional because I believe she doesn't have conscience in the name of medical doctor and she graduated as a licence killer.

For the male students, the orientation is pay 50 thousand and I will give you "A" Alpha. If you didn't meet up big problem huh. Each paper must be sorted out. Days are gone when hard work is being credited. How can we stop crime like this?

Brain Robbing (Internet Fraud)

When we started I told you that good and bad works together for good and you were wondering how of which I made it cleared to you when we were discussing about MR TROUBLE AND MR PROBLEM. Now internet was built in other to facilitate our works and assignments in the office and at home as well because it was made to serve so many purposes but its main purpose was to bring the globe together as a common small village. What is the good news behind internet?

1. Web site
2. Electronic mail services (E-mail),

3. Multimedia message services (mms),
4. Social network such as face book, Google chat etc.

Let me move direct to what I am pointing at. You may say all these listed how can my fellow robbers use them, right? Only if you would say so or ask like that then ask how someone can use a knife meant for kitchen use to killing someone. You know very well that kitchen is where we prepare our daily food and food is necessary to our body so what is the possibility of converting it to a killer material? Wait I am coming one thing about education is that when you stop learning you start dying. Yes education is said to be the means where we get knowledge and the said knowledge is power. But how can knowledge become power if it is not well utilized?

Knowledge becomes power if it is utilized whether properly or not, once there is use in the activity positively or negatively that is when you can say it is power. I believe that the same so called environment or arena of learning where the police, teachers, the robbers, my fellow robber Mr. GOVERNORS all manner of personals went to obtain knowledge.

However before I proceed, I will tell you a small short story about Mr. Brain robber and Mr. Security officer.

Once upon a time, Osogeme and Ire math were in the same university at the same time studying the same course information technology (info Tech) you can as well say (it) remember that I told you that even Mr. lecturer was also among the robbers because he robs in his office now he is teaching Osogeme and Ire math it mean that the all the robbing are interconnected no matter how you look at it. During their stay in the university they both had so many topics base on (info-tech) to obtain a certain degree of knowledge that will bring transformation to the society in general. They were thought to the society in general. They were thought how to make use of face book as one of the social network. They were thought how to make use of Google to get whatever thing they want in this world. Same said Google is where you get the e-mail extractor that you use to extract e-mails. You can use the Google to fish act someone's address, emails etc. Get whatever answer that will cost you an assistant time to get. You can use Google to get news that supposed to be and the pepper. Tell me what you can't find in a Google? All these were made for the benefit of me and you as in to our advantage not disadvantage.

Website: what do we use it for? Website is just creating your home on the web for the world to see. We use the website to make our business known in the world. With the website, you don't need to tell the customer to come to your shop or company before he will know or see what you are into. So, with the help of the website, anyone that needs your services from any part of the world can easy meet with you online together with the way you operate. The website means tell the world about yourself and what you are into: it means going beyond your locality because internet had brought the world to be a common small village.

The website is beyond having a sign post of your business.

What about E-mail i.e. (electronic mail)? Yes it was a truth that before email came to be, we were having and have been writing letters and posting. Yester years, if someone wants to write a letter to you may be you are in Ghana and the other fellow is in Canada, you have to undergo so many protocols just to send a letter. You will count how many days it would take before it gets there only. After which when the email was introduced to us, the letter that ought to take 2 days or whatever is taking only but a second imagine technology. Just create an e-mail ID which is free of cost and it is also privatized by you because it only you that has the pass word no other person. You can save billions of mails sent to you even the ones you sent to others before this age of letters you were able to save which was on broad copy. But you could save as many as e-mails as you can save no matter what. Even if your house or office is destroyed abruptly you could easily log in another computer and restore all mails. Imagine technology? Wonderful. This e-mail service was made to fasten the delivery of mails and create convenience to humanity.

People say that I can talk to my friends all over the world without paying any much through social network E.G face book. Yes it is true. Social network helps to put people together as a common club. When we enter inside the chat room we talk to our friends. However the lecturer thought Osogeme and Iremeth the use of all these and its importance even beyond to the extent of teaching them so many programming languages. The lecturer thought them ethical hacking. How to build walls and destroy walls of security in the banks and big companies. These students were thought so many things of which they graduated with first class honours...waooooo! What a good result! But it doesn't end there. We all know that Osogeme and Iremeth couldn't eat the certificate but should use the knowledge acquired to work anywhere. I must tell this now: whatever thing you do for someone as a service and it is pays you whether daily or weekly or monthly is a job. Okay. Now Iremeth because he had his uncle working in the banking sector and he was given a job so easily immediately they graduated from school. he was put to the security department in the bank to work as there software security manager three years afterwards Iremeth was now a big and rich man just working for three years in that office, he bought a jeep and built a house and got married and Osogeme hasn't got job since that time still helpless. It really made Osogeme sad. Furthermore Osogeme greatest surprise was that the set after their graduation got better jobs and because of their contacts even those that read religious knowledge got job in a bank. These made Osogeme to say to himself that he must convert what he knows as a means of getting money no matter whose detriment it will be...

Now Osogeme decided to be a brain robber!! Osogeme started making use of what he was thought at school to operate until one day he was able to hack in one man's account like that and pulled out $20,000,000 twenty million dollar from the man's bank account. After eight months passed, he was able to build a big company and bought flirt of cars which made everybody astonished.

However, immediately Osogame finished buying these push flirt of cars, EFCC arrested him saying that the money coming into his account needs questioning. How come $10,000,000 ten million dollars in his account in a space of one month? How did he come about that? The EFCC asked about what he does this and that questions arose just to make sure they collect their share if not all.

Before you could know it EFCC confiscated his company. Waooooo that's super and nice. Thank God for EFCC the only organization formed by a group of authority robbers to retrieve those money stolen by those their crime can be easily prosecuted and also those government robbers and individuals that doesn't have enough immunity from the government. Kudus for arresting some governors who didn't pay tithe to you and they people that organized you guys I love your work so much because you guys are really bringing back the lost sheep as in cash that was lost. God bless you for getting down those governors who doesn't know that they should pay their tithe from the whole cash the collected. Also those that escape the probe should go and give thanksgiving for God had covered your eyes not to see them because they paid their quota to you guy.

You are a brain robber. You don't like loop holes yet you are doing your own in the name of retrieving the stolen cash... You are same with our bigger robber Mr. governor. Mr. EFCC you told us how much realize from the said captured criminals but you didn't tell us what the money was used for or that one is not necessary to let us know or tell us where the money was dumped, which wale house or was it transferred as usual to foreign land like other idol cash over there doing nothing instead of using it to certified the need it was used against? Mind you that I didn't say anything ooh because tomorrow you might decide to come after me. What I asked was a question oooh. Why I was saying this is because if those said amount retrieved from those ones pay their quota and we were not told where the money is or what it was used for or the hope of the money to the citizen it means that the money was stolen to be stolen by higher robbers.. FELLA KUTI one of the famous musicians in AFRICA said: INTERNATIONAL THIEF but nobody understood him. But I called mine: THIEF THIEFING THIEF.

Didn't say anything or you call it robbing gentlemen on suit... Not you Ooh. Are you telling me that all those guys coming out for presidential seat and senatorial seat are really coming to serve the nation or are the coming to share the money that remains and maybe finally put us in perpetual debt? I am fully suspecting that one wearing red and black. He looks like one who can put us in a perpetual bankruptcy and debt servicing from the World Bank maybe until my Jesus comes.

Please be careful and arrest him now for questioning otherwise his fellow robber will ring the election and put him there and you know once he enters he has full authority to do an undo and wait for you when he gets down for you to recover the one you thing you can recover maybe 5% of the money he stole you will be able to recover because if you could recover up to 50% of their cash I wonder what will give a woman the effrontery to make a comment that no matter how much the EFCC collect from them in the name of retrieving the nation stolen money that they can't be as poor as DANKOTE GROUP OF COMPANIES.' Mark that word because it's very heavy to the ear. You may deny that you didn't understand what she meant by that statement until it becomes something else… That means we ought to remove the hand of monkey in the pot of soup before it becomes human hand!

Yes if we see human hand in a pot of soup we may not eat it. It is not good if you had diagnosed a patient and found out that he or she is suffering from diabetics now instead of giving him or her insulin as to help the situation and you are giving him or her paracetamol when we know that the paracetamol is for fever. It doesn't show that you are a good doctor when you do that.

Please do the needful because BRAIN ROBBERS are all around you now.

We love you Mr. EFCC but try and probe that one on red and white there. So funny, the white certified him to be pure but eeeh that red colour is a sign of danger. Danger in the house…he is a loin in a sheep wear. I know you get the information that I am passing? Check very well about 85% of them are BRAIN ROBBERS that the reason why the citizens are in trouble and will be in more trouble if nothing is done about the issue and he enters in there.

It seems I am talking about EFCC what about the (NDEA) DRUG ENFORMENT AGENCY?

Out of frustration Duke De Don decided to make it in life and was carrying drugs. I never said that drug trafficking is good but see through my view now. We are discussing this to see how to minimize crime in our society.

When he succeeded making money through this means, he built hotels and hospitals and one private university what our BIGGER ROBBER MR GOVERNOR couldn't build for the benefit of the citizenry and the nation as a whole yes agreed that drug trafficking is contraband but Duke de don was caught with 20 twenty bags of drugs and because of it confiscated his properties. If I may ask who is Mr. Government? Is it not me and you?

Now where is Duke de don? Ooohh in your custody in the name of investigation? You caught him in the name that you were wearing uniform yet you guys are doing the same thing that you accused him of.

The question is who will now arrest you for your crime? The drug you claimed you caught him with was 20 twenty bags of drugs and you boldly show the citizens that Duke de don was apprehended with 3 three bags of drugs. woo that's interesting. What happened to the rest bags? You resell them… It's not the issue but to another dealer like him you did in the same black market. It means that your own activity is robbing Peter to pay Paul. SO how can you stop crime? Don't forget it's a question?

Look at the custom officer? Nicely dressed like a criminal gentlemen on uniform. Could you tell the world what exactly you are doing with that uniform?

Enriching with other people's sweat and you think you could help stop crime? I know one custom officer when come to his house its decorated with cars and jeeps. just take a look at this now, Emeka imported cars from abroad and you make stories that its more than ten year old therefore was seized by you. When you seize it I suppose you bone the cars as something that the country doesn't need at all so that the citizenry will know that it ought not to be rode on the roads of our country but you didn't do it instead you took the best from them all as the boss and kept in your house then the other officer took his own and the other one took his own. Now you succeeded to share the guys sweat and the worse is that you are riding it on the same roads of our country. Now how can you stop crime? Are you not a uniform robber?

26. HOW CAREFUL CAN A MAN BE??

CAREFULNESS: The trait of being cautious; being attentive to possible danger. It is also taking precaution to its full measure in other to avert certain occurrence not to occur. It is good to be careful because a careful man gets to the pick of success. To the understanding of men, a careful man runs away from at least 70% of the bad occurrence. The question is that: is this saying truth? Don't worry you will understand me as we proceed. A fool says there is no god. How could you have said that there is no god? Tell me it was a slip of tongue, because I wonder why you could look around the earth that you are seeing and say there is no god. Have you ever sat down to seeing the cloud the sky, the wind, sun, moon, stars, land, seas, the vegetation, animals and then you? How carefully and wonderfully they were made. I am still on my questions. Tell me Mr. careful, how careful can a man be? It is only God who is careful. Don't allow anyone deceive you that your carefulness can save you. If you think that you are careful there are millions of men out there who are more careful than you do still make mistakes and fall. It is only God who is careful. A doctor whom we assumed that they are professionals and as a professional he is we expect him to be careful in terms of taking care of us when we are sick. Just imagine that a patient was brought to the hospital for doctor to do surgery on him and upon how we trusted the doctor's carefulness believing in his profession still forgot surgery blade inside the patients' stomach. Upon how careful he was trained to be as a life saver and the patient gave up a ghost lastly it was found that the surgery blade was left in the stomach of the patient. If that patient were to be your brother or sister, what could you have done to the doctor? How careful can a man be?

A boy and a girl was dating and unfortunately the started seeing each other one day the girl noticed some advances from the boy and she told him that she wouldn't like him to do anything stupid with her as in trying to sleep with rather say make love to her because she was afraid of pregnancy. On a very good day both of them happened to be together and one thing lead to another they had it and afterwards nothing happened. Okay now were they both not careful? "Yes" they were and because of the success of the success of yesterday activity both had another one in agreement that they world wear protective measure in other to avoid pregnancy. The truth remains that it was like that in their careful eyes but the third time they had it and the boy was wearing two protectives this time around thinking that it shows more than carefulness and low and behold after the show the girl couldn't see herself the next month that there was every tendency that she could be pregnant. Telling the smart boy what happened they both decided to go for lab test at the hospital and the result was positive! Hay girl shouted how could this happen when you were wearing two protective? Boy said my dear, I don't know ooh. Girl said you don't know what? I told you to be careful and you promised that you would now in which way were you careful about this boy said I am sorry dear, it wasn't my fault. Girl said whose fault then? Boy answered what exactly are we going to do now? I think termination is the option here now girl said what do you mean? Can you trust the doctor to carefully terminate it without issues? Boy said don't worry my dear the doctor is trained for that and will carefully and professionally do it. Now the girl agreed and after the doctor finished their girl gave her ghost. You see Mrs. careful died thinking that she was careful. How careful can a man be?

One day one man told me that he was too careful couple with his intelligence to make mistakes in his company. I told him that it was a careless and foolish talk that he just made. How careful can you possibly be? Now look at the person that said he was too careful to make mistake. This man has a company worth of $50,000,000. 50 million dollar and he collected loan from the bank worth 10 million dollars and was doing very well in his business. One day a contract was awarded to one foreigner for the company expansion. When the expansion contractors where through and he was asked to write a cheque of $1,000,000 one million dollars for the done deal and decides he was the one who had the negotiation with the foreign contractors and he carelessly put a cheque of $100,000,000 one hundred million dollars and signed by him. Now the foreign contractor saw this and shouted wow and never said anything until the cheque was cleared. Besides the difference in this was just mere zero and added ignorance by him. The foreign contractor takes it as how God can bless one overnight.

This is just money that they would have made in 10 contracts but they got it in 1 contract. They ran away with the money. Still at the carelessly signed that money he never found out until the bank came to collect the loan back that year and he found out that he was unable to pay the bank and if he didn't pay his company would be seized and he would be left with nothing. He calls for account auditing and it was revealed he was the one who signed out that money through his cheque book to foreign contractor. When he heard that it was him who did the signing he collapsed and died. Just look at upon how careful that man claimed to be but he was careless to sign a cheque that cost his company.

How careful can a man be? Doctors are trained to be careful and upon how careful they were trained to be, or to take care of life, people die in their hands.

Soldiers put protective measure to war by wearing bullet proof and yet soldiers with those entire bullets proof die at the war front. How careful can a man be?

No matter how you try or claim to be careful if you don't have Jesus, I wonder where you carefulness will lead you to. Just look at the short stories about so many who told claimed that carefulness of theirs. When you think that you are too careful it gives you one stupid one can do mentality and things spoil. Anytime your mind is telling you that you are careful, look very well before you fall. No one is careful in life. If man is careful nothing could have killed man. At he was not careful yet that small thing that killed him. The question is why did he die? I thought he was careful but how careful he is? His carefulness could have been on that small thing that led to his death yet he died. What a pity. Death for example is inevitable no matter how careful you are death is inevitable. A lady spent some thousands of dollars in abroad for skill surgery rubbing expensive cream on skill to make it glow morning and night. In fact the kind of perfume she uses in the morning is the different from the one in afternoon and also night imagine just two keep her skin glowing. But the question is why didn't she be careful to avoid Mr. Death when he comes to kill her? At least she could have explained to Mr. Death that she spent a lot of money on that her skin. If she had known she couldn't have gone to her last surgery that killed her. How careful can a man be?

27. TIME

Time is a rare luxury which can never be purchase at any cost so if and when someone spends it for you, it defines the depth of come they have for you. According to new Pocket Oxford English Dictionary: time is the unlimited continued progress of existence and events in the past present and future. It points to a point or period of time.

Time is the only main thing that comes and goes. Time is very important with its season and periods. If time is not well utilized, that is when people say: "if I had known, I would have done this and that when the time is no longer. Time waits for nobody and the worse is that it does not respect or fear anyone. The only neither man that fears nor respect no personality. Time is money and there is nothing like game of luck towards mama success. Everything is time and chance for you to make it. E.g. look at this short joke.

A man always come late to everything both important and less important ones was it not one day it happened when where he was supposed to be on time in a special meeting and he took Mr. time so carefully and time casual zed his chances of seeing Mr. opportunity and mama success. On that day he supposed to represent his people in that which the supposed to get a contract of $500,000,000 (five hundred million dollars) to their zone because it was their turn and he was the one representing their zone. Mr. Time to prove to him that him (time) doesn't wait for anybody. The man came late usual. Do you know that before he come the men who supposed to give the contract waited and they changed their mind to giving the contract to another person from another zone! When the man arrives, he never knew that the contract had been handed over to another man from another zone not even his zone. As the meeting was about to end still no discussion about the contract then be began to asking if the men who is to award the contract didn't come again. Lo and behold he was told that the deal had been done. He said: "how?" he supposed to be the person it was due to be given to them? The speaker said to him that he came late besides the deal ought to be done. They men for the contract waited and waited and they decide to give it to another fellow because the deal ought to be done and they had no much time to spend. The man said to the speaker: "how do you mean?" was it not some minutes late that I was to the meeting? Medicine after death says the speaker. Those men you saw when you were entering were the men. They said that they couldn't spend much time so they did and left.

Don't waste time on anything because any second is money. One second is very dangerous. On second is what winners use to win. One second cost you a hundred million dollar like it did to this man. Yes who knows whether the profit he could have gotten from that contract could be more than $100,000,000 (one hundred million dollars.)

Everything God made were made base on their seasons (time). There are season for all trees anyone you force to produce outside its season always have side effect nutritionally.

There is a time for everything: and a season for every activity under the heavens a time to be born and a time to die.

A time to plant and a time to up root.

A time to plant and a time to up

A time to kill and a time to heal.

A time to tear down and a time to build.

A time to weep and a time to laugh.

A time to mourn and a time to dance.

A time to scatter stones and a time to gather them.

A time to embrace and a time to refrain from embracing.

A time to search and a time to give up.

A time to tear and a time to mend.

A time to be silent and a time to speak.

A time to love and a time to hate.

A time for war and a time for peace.

Whoever obeys the time will come to no harm and the wise heart will know the proper Time and procedure. For there is always a proper time and procedure for every matter, though a person may be weighed down by misery. Since no one knows the future who calls tell someone else what is to come? As no one has power over the wind to contain it, so no one has power over the time of their death. As no one is discharged in time of war so wickedness will not release those who practice it.

Make every day count because there is no extra time in a day. You cannot change yesterday but you can do something today that can change tomorrow. It doesn't matter how you were born remember that was time yesterday. It doesn't matter what happened last ten years or last fifteen years ago you may not be able to change it but you can reposition yourself today. You can make a decision today that will change what tomorrow will bring. Invest in your future.. Refuse to be ordinary. Refuse to end your life on management or on a side work. I believe if you act on what I am communicating to you it will change your future. Noon was born to be poor. You may have born poor but you were not born to be poor. You may have been brought up poor but you are not brought up to be poor. The definition of adulthood is responsibility. When you become an adult you become responsible. You become responsibility for you future. What do you have in yourself? Bring it out the world needs it to move forward otherwise the world will be complete without your contribution you know why? God deposited something inside of everyone. There are many who cry for help because there was no answer for their call for help the feel the pains of neglects. No my dear refuse to give up Believe in everything that God made. God made you and He never made a failure. Believe that God has a purpose for your life. You may have been born as a parental accident but you were not a divine accident. God knew that you were coming and He made a sufficient provisions for you. There is a place for you in the world.

I want to help you in this book to fine that place. There are many things that you need to do for all these to come to reality. There are things that are not in abundance supply in life. They are limited and one of them is MR TIME. There is no extra TIME in life. Life is not a game. Therefore make every day count for your life. Improve yourself every day. Introduce something into your life that counts. Choose to be a success. Become inspiring. Distinguish yourself with character and excellence. If you are a singer be a singer with a difference. Put yourself and your best into everything that you and change your world. Do it the best way for the first time. TIME is important. Success is waiting for the man who makes decisions. Do not spend your TIME watching videos and TV every day. Those that you are watching put their best TIME in to what you are watching. It's high time you change the position and put yourself there to be watched. Tell yourself: I WILL BE WATCHED! You hear men brag with other peoples products. They can seat down at a place and tell you the names of all the products in the world. They brag about designers but the question is, where is your own product and designs for others to make use of? Challenge yourself today for the future. There is no place for you at the top. Give yourself to a teacher and train your mind and use it. If you train your mind it will be ready to deliver to you the right thought and ideas that will earn you a commercial values. There is no poverty for a man you has made an investment to his mind and he willing to act. There is no hunger for the man who train his mind to think through on every problem to solve every problem. Train yourself to think through problems and bring out solution let men come to you for advise.

Decide to be smart. Decide to be a problem solver. If you make that decision that is what you will be. Problem solver are in short supply in the world. There is a place for a man who choose to be one today. Engage yourself national and international issues. Get involved. Get concern. There are many best singers and writers in the world the question is, where are their writings and songs? Maybe they lavish TIME in sleeping, or they playing too much, or resting too much. Its hightime you started using your TIME properly to change your world.

When a bird is alive it eats ants. When a bird dies ants eats the bird. Time and circumstance can change at any time. Don't devalue or hurt anyone in life. You may be powerful today but remember, time is more powerful than you! One tree makes a million match sticks, but when the time comes, one match stick is needed to burn a million trees. Let's encourage one another to sets of kindness.

Don't forget a second is just like one million years you can't measure the immediate past one second. The distance is too far! You as well can't remember exactly what happened in the last part immediate one second. One second is tomorrow and that same one. Time is money.